Keto Bread Machine, (Dessert [4 books in 1]

How to Cheat Without Getting Caught!

By

Keto Flex Academy

Table of Contents

Keto Bread Machine Cookbook 2021 with Pictures

Keto Bread and Keto Snacks

Keto Dessert & Chaffle Cookbook 2021 with Pictures

The Complete Ketogenic Guidebook for Women Over 50

Keto Bread Machine Cookbook 2021 with Pictures

By

Keto Flex Academy

Table of Contents

Introduction

Bread is the most prominent food in almost every household around the globe. Bread is commonly a product of baking consists of numerous kinds of doughs, buns, and crusts. Usually, all kinds of bread dough are made from flour, yeast, and water in different shapes, methods, and flavors. The main process evolves around mixing and blending until they turned into a rigid paste or dough and then baked into a bread, loaf, or bun form afterward.

If we go through history, we will see that bread is one of the oldest food made and consumed by human beings since the beginning of agriculture. It plays a noteworthy role in religious rituals and cultural life, and language. Bread has a lot of significant roles as a meal around the world. It is consumed differently in different cultures, most often as a side meal, snacks, breakfast, lunch, or dinner or even combined as an important ingredient in different food/cuisine preparations.

Freshly homemade bread is one of the most satisfying things to eat and make. Although because of hectic life routines and busy schedules, most people have never even tried making homemade bread in their lives. But a lot has begun to change with the arrival of automatic bread machines you can easily make bread at the convenience of your home without spending a lot of time.

One of the best things about making your homemade bread is that you can always opt for healthy ingredients; unlike bread, you buy from outside when you make homemade fresh bread. You can always customize your list of ingredients, be it nuts of your choice, almond or coconut flour, gluten-free bread, nutritional yeast, or any other sort of restrictive ingredients.

Now the main question arises what a bread machine is? How does the bread machine work? How many kinds of bread can you make with a bread machine? Or is the bread machine worth buying?

An automatic home appliance for turning uncooked ingredients into dough or baked bread is called a bread machine. A bread machine is made up of a baking pan, built-in paddles at the bottom of the pan seated in a small oven center. The bread machine usually comes up with a small built-in screen called a control panel. You can adjust your choice of preferences while baking bread using settings input via the control panel.

Usually, the different bread machine comes up with different instructions. It may take some time to read the full instructions of your machine. But you will get a whole idea about the operating, cleaning, and safety features of the machine. Besides operating and other options manual will also provide a selection of recipes that are tested. If you are new to breadmaking, these recipes particularly are an excellent way to start.

The traditional order of ingredients starts with liquids and finishes with the dry ingredients, the fat, and then the yeast, though there may be some exceptions. The yeast is held away from the fluids not to activate until it starts to knead.

There are many different programs for producing many different styles of the loaf for most bread makers. Using various types of flour and varying the other ingredients, you can produce white bread, pizza whole meal, or special loaves. On its display screen, you can see the numerous choices this beadmaker offers (from the top: basic, whole meal, multigrain, French, pizza, cake, dough, and bake only). You put a slightly different mix into the tin at the beginning for different breads and choose a different program from the show. The bread machine can automatically manage various kneading, growing and baking times, and so on. You can use the bread machine to make different kinds of dough by choosing the dough cycle option from the control panel then baking it in the oven in any shape or form you like. From bun to baguettes, to pizza pull-apart, if you prefer a particular shape or bread style.

Nowadays bread machine is a very helpful and essential tool for most busy people. It has transformed baking bread into a hand-off process. From kneading to baking, the bread machine does all the job. Just measure and put all the ingredients in the baking pan, close the lid, start the button, and you are done. It feels magical if you own a bread machine. Without any extra effort, you can enjoy fresh homemade bread any day or at any time of the week, and it is worth investing your money in.

Chapter 1: Bread Machine Breakfast Recipes

1.1 Simple Flaxseed Keto Bread

Total time of cooking

3 hours 10 minute

Servings

5

Nutrition facts

Calories 263 (for two slices)

Fat 18g

Protein 12g

Net carbs 4g

fiber 10g

total carbs 14g

Ingredients:

This is the list of ingredients required to make simple flaxseeds keto bread.

- 1 cup of almond flour

- 1/4 cup of brown flaxseeds

- 1/3 cup of coconut flour

- 1 teaspoon of active dry yeast

- 2 tablespoons of psyllium husk powder

- 1/2 teaspoon of baking soda

- 1/2 teaspoon of salt

- 3 egg whites

- 1 whole egg

- 1 cup of warm water

- 1 teaspoon of olive oil

Instructions:

Follow the instructions mentioned below to make flaxseeds keto bread.

1. Sift the flour first to remove lumps.

2. First, add warm water to the bread machine pan, and sprinkle active dry yeast on top

   .

3. Wait for the yeast to activate.

4. Approximately After 5 minutes, add all the other ingredients into the bread machine pan.

5. Press the basic cycle option from your bread machine and choose medium crust.

6. When baking is finished, wait for few minutes before you remove bread from the pan.

7. slice and enjoy

1.2 Keto Coconut white bread (grain, gluten, and sugarfree)

Total time of cooking

3 hours 50 minutes

Servings

20 servings

Nutrition facts

Calories 56 (per serving)

Fat 4g

Protein 2.4g

Net carbs 1.2g

Ingredients:

Here is the list of ingredients required to make keto coconut white bread.

- 1 1/2 (180g) cups of almond flour

- 7 large eggs at room temperature

- 3 tablespoon (43 g) of apple cider vinegar

- 3.75 tablespoon (33g) of finely grounded psyllium husk powder

- 4 teaspoon (12g) of instant yeast

- 1 1/2 (360g) of lukewarm water

- 4 teaspoon (18g) of baking powder

- 1 teaspoon of salt

- 3 tablespoon (45g) of olive or coconut oil optional

Instructions:

Follow the instructions mentioned below to make keto coconut white bread.

1. Assemble all the ingredients.

2. Place the kneading paddles in the bread machine pan.

3. Follow your bread machine recommended order and add all of the above ingredients. Sprinkle yeast on top of the ingredients to ensure that it does not come into contact with other liquid ingredients.

4. Choose gluten-free and medium crust in the settings press the start button.

5. When the baking time is over, click the stop button.

6. Remove the baking pan from the bread machine to cool down for a while before removing the bread.

7. After a while, when it is cooled down, give your baking pan a toss and slightly remove bread from the pan.

8. bread is ready to serve.

1.3 Light and fluffy keto flaxseed buns

Total time of cooking

55 minutes

Servings

4 servings

Nutrition facts

Calories 232 (per serving)

Fat 11.9g

Protein 10.6g

Fiber 13.6g

Net carbs 2.1

Total carbs 15.7g

Ingredients:

Here is the list of ingredients required to make light and fluffy keto flaxseed buns.

- 1 1/4 (150g) cups of golden grounded flaxseeds

- 4 large egg whites or 2 whole egg at room temperature

- 2 tablespoon (28 g) of apple cider vinegar

- 1 teaspoon of psyllium powder

- 1/4 to 1 teaspoon of salt

- 2 teaspoon (8g) of baking powder

- 50 ml/0.2 cup of hot boiling water

Instructions:

Follow the instructions mentioned below to make light and fluffy keto flaxseed buns

1. Assemble all the ingredients.

2. As recommended by your bread machine, add all of the above ingredients. Add water, apple cider vinegar, golden flaxseeds grounded, psyllium powder, eggs, baking powder, and salt.

3. Choose the dough cycle option from the settings and press the start button.

4. When the dough cycle is over, click the stop button.

5. Remove the dough from the bread pan and divide the dough into 90 g portions each evenly. You will have more buns if you will make smaller portions.

6. Turn on the oven. At 350 F or 180 C, preheat your oven.

7. As the dough is sticky, so make sure to wet your hands before shaping it into balls. Now make balls and place them over a baking tray lined with parchment paper.

8. Sprinkle the top of the bun with seeds or herbs of your choice.

9. Place the baking tray in the oven. And bake for around 30 minutes or until golden brown. Touch and see if buns feel light and hollow upon touching it's done.

10. Remove from oven and serve.

1.4 Keto banana almond bread

Total time of cooking

4 hours

Servings

12 servings

Nutrition facts

Calories 173 (per serving)

Fiber 2.5g

Protein 3.9g

Net carbs 2.3g

Fat 14.9g

Ingredients:

Here is the list of ingredients required to make keto banana almond bread.

- 3/4 (84g) cups of coconut flour

- 1/2 (120ml) cups of heavy whipping cream at room temperature

- 1/2 cup + 1 tablespoon (130g) melted unsalted butter at room temperature

- 5 large eggs at room temperature

- 1/2 (100g) cup of granulated sweetener

- 2 teaspoons (10 ml) of banana extract

- 1/4 teaspoon (1g) of salt

- 2 teaspoons (8g) of baking powder

- 1 teaspoon (3g) of ground cinnamon

- 1 teaspoon (5ml) of vanilla extract

- 1 cup of chopped almonds

Instructions:

Follow the instructions mentioned below to make keto banana almond bread.

1. Assemble all the ingredients.

2. As suggested by your bread machine, add all of the above ingredients in the bread machine baking pan except almonds.

3. Check dough after 5 minutes. If required, add 1 to 2 tbsp of water or flour according to the consistency of the dough.

4. When the machine beep, add almonds 5 to 10 minutes before the kneading cycle completes.

5. Choose the baking option according to the instructions of your bread machine.

6. Select the loaf size and crust color from the bread machine settings.

7. Once the baking is completed, transfer the bread into the oven rack and let it cool down for some time.

8. Cut into slices, top up with your favorite keto low carb syrup and enjoy.

1.5 Easy Keto Egg Loaf(How to make a keto French toast from an egg loaf)

Total time of cooking

55 minutes

Servings

4

Nutrition facts

Calories 232(per slice for egg loaf only)

Protein 5.7g

Net carbs 2.5g

Fat 20.6g

Ingredients:

Here is the list of ingredients required to make keto egg loaf.

- 4 tablespoons of melted butter

- 1/4 cup of coconut flour

- 4 whole eggs

- 8 oz cream cheese

- 3 tablespoons of any sweetener of your choice

- 1/4 cup of heavy whipping cream

- 2 teaspoons of baking powder

- 1 teaspoon of vanilla extract

- 1 teaspoon of cinnamon powder

Ingredients for keto French toast egg dip:

- 2 medium-sized eggs

- 1/2 tablespoon or 8 grams of unsweetened vanilla almond milk

- 1/2 tablespoon or 8 grams of keto maple syrup

- pinch of cinnamon powder

Instructions:

Follow the instructions mentioned below to make keto egg loaf

1. Put all the egg loaf ingredients in the bread machine pan, select the dough option from your bread machine menu and press the start button. After five minutes, check the dough if water or flour is needed.

2. Lined loaf pan with parchment paper, pour the egg loaf mixture into loaf pan and even out the top surface of egg loaf with a spatula's help.

3. Bake an egg loaf at 350 f for around 45 minutes or check with a toothpick.

4. Remove the loaf from the pan.

5. Before cutting it into slices, let the bread cool down on the baking rack for a while.

   Instructions to make French toast egg dip

6. Take a small-size mixing bowl and break two medium eggs in it.

7. Add 1/2 tablespoon of unsweetened vanilla almond milk, 1/2 tablespoon of keto maple syrup, and a pinch of powdered cinnamon. Whisk with a fork until eggs are fully combined with other ingredients.

8. Dip the bread slices one by one into egg dip from both sides.

9. Turn on the stove and place the pan over medium heat, coat it with baking spray and cook bread from both sides until crispy or golden brown.

10. Serve your French toast with fruits and keto maple syrup.

1.6 Low Carb Keto Bagels

Total time of cooking

45 minutes

Servings

8

Nutrition facts

Calories 298(per bagel)

Protein 18g

Net carbs 5g

Fat 23g

Ingredients:

Here is the list of ingredients required to make keto bagels.

- 3 cups of shredded mozzarella cheese

- 2 oz cream cheese

- 3 large eggs (reserved one egg for egg wash)

- 1 1/3 cup of almond flour

- 1 tablespoon of baking powder

- for topping sesame seeds cheese or bagel seasoning (optional)

Instructions:

Follow the method mentioned below to make low-carb keto bagels.

1.Assemble all the ingredients.

2.In a safe microwave bowl, melt together mozzarella and cream cheese in 30 second intervals. Check after every 30 seconds, stir until cheese is completely melted. You can also melt cheese in a double boiler over the burner.

3.Now, place all the ingredients, including melted cheese, in the bread machine pan, select dough from settings, and press the start button.

4.Once the dough cycle is finished, take the dough out of the bread machine. The dough will be very adhering, which is ok.

5.Wrap pastry board with plastic wrap. Coat your hands with oil, and divide your dough into 8 equal sections. Now roll each dough section on the pastry board to make 1-inch thick dough ropes. The plastic wrap will prevent your dough from sticking to the board.

6.Make the circle shape with a 1-inch thick rope and pinch the ends shut.

7.Place bagels carefully on a baking sheet lined with parchment paper .place each bagel from a distance of 1 inch at least.

8.Now coat the top surface of bagels with an egg wash at this stage. If you want to add any bagel toppings, you can.

9.In a preheated oven, bake the bagels in the middle rack of the oven for around 14 to 15 minutes or until it turns golden brown.

10.Before removing it from the baking tray, allow the bagels to cool down.

1.7 Keto Raspberry and Lemon Loaf(grain, sugar, and gluten-free)

Total time of cooking

4 hours

Servings

12

Nutrition facts

Calories 166 (per slice)

Protein 5.7g

Fiber 2.5g

Net carbs 2.8g

Fat 14.7g

Ingredients:

Here is the list of ingredients required to make keto raspberry and lemon loaf.

- 4 tablespoons of sour cream

- 4 tablespoons of melted butter

- 2 whole eggs

- 200 grams of almond flour

- 1.5 teaspoon of baking powder

- 1 teaspoon of lemon essence/extract.

- 1 teaspoon of vanilla extract

- 1/4 cup of sugar substitute

- 100 grams of raspberries halved

Instructions:

Follow the method mentioned below to make keto raspberry and lemon loaf.

1.Assemble all the ingredients.

2.In the bread machine pan, add all the ingredients except raspberries and select the basic setting for bread and medium crust color, press start.

3.Prior to 5 minutes before the kneading cycle finishes, add raspberries(your machine will beep as a signal).

4.Bread machine will beep once the baking is done.

5.Remove bread pan from baking machine. Turn the bread pan upside down, give it a toss to remove bread easily place on baking rack let it cool down for few minutes before slicing.

6.serve.

1.8 Keto Peanut Butter Donut Recipe(grain, sugar, and gluten-free)

Total time of cooking

45 minutes

Servings

8

Nutrition facts

Calories 175 (per donut)

Protein 7g

Carbs 5g

Fiber 2g

Net carbs 3

Fat 14g

Ingredients:

Here is the list of ingredients required to make a keto peanut butter donut recipe.

- 1 and 1/4 cup of almond flour

- 1/2 cup of sugar substitute

- 1/3 cup and 2 tablespoons of unsweetened vanilla almond milk

- 5 tablespoons of no sugar added peanut butter

- 2 large eggs

- 1 teaspoon of baking powder

- 1/2 teaspoon of vanilla extract

- pinch of salt

For donut glaze

- 4 tablespoons of powdered peanut butter

- 3/4 tablespoon of confectioners' sugar

- 2 1/2 tablespoon of water

Instructions:

Follow the method mentioned below to make keto peanut butter donuts.

1. Assemble all the ingredients.

2.In the bread machine pan, add all the ingredients except unsweetened vanilla almond milk in the order mentioned by your bread machine—select the dough option from the control panel and press the start button.

3.Place dough in a large mixing bowl and add 1/3 cup of unsweetened vanilla almond milk. Fold it in the batter until it combines with dough and pourable batter forms.

4.Coat a donut pan with baking spray and pour the batter into the donut tray.

5.Place donut pan in the oven bake at 350 f for around 15 to 16 minutes.

6.Remove the donut pan out of the oven and let them cool down for few minutes.

Instructions for donut glaze:

1.For a donut glaze, add powdered peanut butter, confectioner sugar, and water in a bowl.

2.Mix well until a thick peanut butter glaze starts to form.

3.Add glaze layer on a donut.

4.Add toppings of your choice over donut glaze (you can use crushed peanuts or no-sugar-added chocolate chips.

1.9 Easy and Yummy Keto Blueberry Bread

Total time of cooking

5 hours

Servings

6

Nutrition facts

Calories 216 (per slice)

Protein 6g

Sugar 1g

Carbs 6g

Fiber 2g

Net carbs 4g

Fat 20g

Ingredients:

Here is the list of ingredients required to make a keto blueberry bread

- 1 cup of almond flour blanched

- 1/3 cup of blueberries

- 1/4 cup of coconut oil softened

- 2 large eggs at room temperature

- 1/2 cup of erythritol

- 2 tablespoons of canned coconut milk

- 1 teaspoon of vanilla extract

- 2 teaspoon bread machine yeast

Instructions:

Follow the method mentioned below to make keto blueberry bread.

1.Assemble all the ingredients.

2.In the bread machine pan, add all the ingredients except blueberries in the order mentioned by your bread machine.

3.Choose a basic cycle and medium crust from the settings.

4.Add blueberries when the bread machine beep, around five minutes before kneading completes.

5.Let it bake until the machine beeps.

6.When done, take out bread from the baking pan carefully and let it cool completely before serving.

7.slice and enjoy.

1.10 Low-Carb Keto Chocolate Breakfast Loaf

Total time of cooking

2 hours 40 minutes

Servings

12

Nutrition facts

Calories 133 (per slice)

Protein 4g

Carbs 5.5g

Fiber 3g

Net carbs 2.5g

Fat 10.5g

Ingredients:

Here is the list of ingredients required to make a low-carb keto chocolate breakfast loaf.

- 6 tablespoons of salted butter

- 4 eggs large

- 1/3 cup heaping full fat sour cream

- 1 1/3 cup almond flour

- 2/3 cup of sugar substitute

- 1/4 cup cocoa powder(unsweetened)

- 1 teaspoon vanilla extract

- 2 1/2 tablespoon keto chocolate chips

- 2 teaspoon instant yeast

Instructions:

Follow the method mentioned below to make low-carb keto chocolate breakfast loaf.

1.Add all the ingredients except chocolate chips to the bread machine pan. Follow the order recommended by your bread machine.

2.choose dough cycle from the settings panel. start press.

3.Add chocolate chips five minutes before the kneading cycle completes. (when the machine beeps as a signal).

4.When the dough cycle ends, remove the dough from the bread machine pan.

5.Coat loaf pan with baking spray and line with parchment paper.

6.Evenly spread the dough into the loaf pan and sprinkle keto chocolate chips at the surface of the loaf.

7.Bake it for around 50 minutes at 350 f in the preheated oven.

8.Insert a toothpick to check if your loaf is raw or done if it comes out clean, your loaf is done.

9.Cool it for a while before slicing.

1.11 Keto Rye Bread

Total time of cooking

2 hours 40 minutes

Servings

18

Nutrition facts

Calories 107 (per slice)

Protein 9.4g

Carbs 1.94g

Fiber 1.66g

Net carbs 7.44g

Fat 5g

Ingredients:

Here is the list of ingredients required to make keto rye bread.

- 1/2 cup of oat fiber

- 2 eggs beaten (at room temperature)

- 1.25 cups of vital wheat gluten

- 1 cup of warm, strong coffee

- 2/3 cup of flaxseed meal

- 2 tablespoons of unsweetened cocoa powder

- 2 tablespoons of erythritol powdered sweetener

- 2 tablespoons of butter(at room temperature)

- 1 tablespoon of caraway and 1 tablespoon of dill seeds

- 1 tablespoon active dry yeast

- 1 teaspoon honey

- 1 teaspoon pink Himalayan salt

- 1/2 teaspoon xanthan gum

Instructions:

Follow the method mentioned below to make keto rye bread.

1.Grab your container out of your bread machine.

2.Add all the ingredients (warm coffee, eggs, oat fiber, flaxseed meal, vital wheat gluten, add salt, erythritol, honey, xanthan gum, and butter around the outside edge of bread container not directly in the middle)now add active dry yeast, make a hole in the middle of dry ingredients, and add active dry yeast in the middle of the little hole to make sure the yeast does not come in contact with liquid ingredients. At the top of the mixture, add cocoa powder, caraway seeds, and dill seeds.

3.Put back the container in the bread machine, close the lid, and select basic white bread settings and dark crust from your machine control panel.

4.When the bread is done, remove it from the pan and cool it for a while on the oven rack.

5. slice and enjoy.

1.12 Soft And Fluffy Keto Walnut And Chocolate bread

Total time of cooking

2 hours 10 minutes

Servings

21

Nutrition facts

Calories 66 (per slice)

Protein 3g

Net carbs 1g

Fat 4.4g

Ingredients:

Here is the list of ingredients required to make walnut and chocolate bread.

- 3/4 cup of coconut flour

- 3/4 golden flaxseed grounded(use coffee bean grinder or multi grinder to make powder)

- 1/2 cup of erythritol

- 1/2 cup of dark chocolate (melted)

- 1/2 cup chopped walnuts(reserved half for topping and half for bread)

- 1 cup of hot water

- 3 tablespoons of psyllium husk powder(grounded in finer texture)

- 3 tablespoons of apple cider vinegar

- 9 large egg whites

- 3 teaspoons of baking powder

- 1 teaspoon of salt

Instructions:

Follow the method mentioned below to make keto walnut and chocolate bread.

1.Assemble all the ingredients.

2.Add all the ingredients except walnuts to the bread machine container in the order suggested by your bread machine.

3.Choose basic dough settings and press the start button. After kneading for few minutes, check the consistency of the dough and add one tablespoon of water or flour if required.

4.Five minutes prior to the last kneading, when the machine beeps, add walnuts.

5.Remove the dough from the pan when the kneading cycle ends.

6.Warmed up your oven at 350 f or 180 c.

7.Coat 8x4 pan lined at the bottom with parchment paper with baking spray. Spread the dough evenly.

8.Coat the top of the bread with chopped walnuts.

9.Bake for around 60 minutes in the preheated oven.

10.Place a wooden skewer in bread to check if it comes out clean it is done.

11.Cool it down on the oven rack before slicing.

12.Serve and enjoy.

1.13 Best Keto Coffee Cake

Total time of cooking

2 hours

Servings

16

Nutrition facts

Calories 167 (per slice)

Protein 3g

Net carbs 2g

Fat 16g

Total carbs 3g

Sugar 1g

Ingredients:

Here is the list of ingredients required to make keto coffee cake.

For the coffee cake batter:

- 1 1/2 cup of almond flour

- 1/2 cup of any keto sweetener

- 1/4 cup of heavy cream or coconut cream

- 1/3 cup of unsweetened almond milk

- 1/2 cup of melted butter or coconut oil

- 4 medium eggs at room temperature

- 2 tablespoons of coconut flour

- 2 teaspoons of baking powder

- 1/4 teaspoon of salt

- 2 teaspoons of vanilla extract

For the crumb topping:

- 1 cup of almond flour

- 1/2 cup of keto powdered sweetener

- 1/4 cup of soft butter or coconut oil

- 1/2 cup of nuts of your choice

- 1 teaspoon of ground cinnamon powder

For the cinnamon sugar:

- 1/4 cup of powdered sweetener

- 1 tablespoon of almond flour

- 1 teaspoon of ground cinnamon powder

For the sugar-free glaze:

- 1/3 cup of powdered erythritol

- 4 to 5 tablespoons of heavy cream

- 1 teaspoon of vanilla extract

Instructions:

Follow the method mentioned below to make keto coffee cake

1.Assemble all the ingredients.

2.Add all the ingredients of the coffee cake batter mentioned in the list into the bread machine container and select dough cycle.

3.During kneading, check the dough add water or flour if required according to the consistency of the dough.

4.When the machine beeps. Remove the dough from the bread machine.

5.At 350 f or 180 c preheat your oven.

6.For Crumb Topping:

Combine all of the crumb topping ingredients with the help of a fork until the mixture becomes crumbly.

7.For Cinnamon Sugar:

Take a bowl and mix together almond flour, ground cinnamon powder, and sweetener. Keep it aside.

8.Line a 9x9 inches square cake pan with parchment paper.

9.For assembling the first spread half of the cake batter to the pan. Now add a layer of cinnamon sugar and then again spread the remaining cake batter. Over the top of the cake, evenly spread crumb mixture.

10.Place the baking pan in preheated oven and bake for around 35 to 40 minutes or until of cake is golden browned.

11. Now, prepare a sugar-free glaze. Mix all the ingredients to make a sugar-free glaze until the glaze thickens, and powdered erythritol is dissolved.

12. Cut the cake into 16 slices and drizzle the glaze over the top of the coffee cake.

13. Serve and enjoy.

1.14 Easy And Tasty Keto Yogurt Cake

Total time of cooking

2 hours 55 minutes

Servings

12

Nutrition facts

Calories 188(per serving)

Protein 7g

Carbs 6g

Fat 16g

Fiber 4g

Ingredients:

Here is the list of ingredients for yogurt bread.

- 2 cups of almond flour

- 1 cup of Greek yogurt

- 1/2 cup of granulated erythritol

- 1/3 cup of melted unsalted butter

- 3 large eggs

- 2 tablespoons of coconut flour

- 1 1/2 tablespoon of lemon juice

- 1 tablespoon of lemon zest

- 2 teaspoons of bread machine yeast

For glaze:

- 1/2 cup of powdered erythritol

- 2 to 3 tablespoons of water

- 1 tablespoon of lemon juice

Instructions:

Follow the method mentioned below to make keto yogurt bread.

1. Assemble all the ingredients.

2. In the bread maker pan, add all the ingredients of lemon bread and choose basic bread and medium crust from the control panel to start the machine.

3. Check the consistency of dough during kneading. If needed, add two tablespoons of water.

4. When the baking cycle ends, place bread on a cooling rack.

5. For the glaze, add powdered erythritol and lemon juice, and water into the bowl mix until all ingredients are well combined.

6. Slice the cooled bread and top up with glaze.

Chapter 2: Bread Machine Lunch Recipes

2.1 Keto Low Carb Naan Flatbread

Total time of cooking

40 minutes

Servings

3

Nutrition facts

Calories 530 (per flatbread naan)

Protein 28g

Carbs 6g

Fat 41g

Fiber 2g

Ingredients:

Here is the list of ingredients required to make keto low carb naan flatbread.

- 1 1/2 and another 1/4 cup of almond flour blanched

- 1 1/2 cups of shredded mozzarella full fat

- 2/3 cup of protein powder unflavored

- 1 egg beaten

- 1 1/2 tablespoons of full-fat sour cream

- 1 teaspoon of baking powder

- pinch of salt

Instructions:

Follow the method mentioned below to make keto low carb naan flatbread.

1.Assemble all the ingredients.

2.In a microwave-proof bowl, add mozzarella and sour cream and melt in 30 seconds of intervals until both ingredients are fully melted down.

3.Place all the ingredients in the bread machine container and select the dough cycle. After five minutes of kneading, check the dough consistency. If needed, add water or flour.

4.When the dough cycle finishes, remove the dough from the container and let the dough rest for 15 to 20 minutes.

5.Once the dough has rested, divide your dough into three portions equally and add water into your hands to prevent dough from sticking into your fingers.

6.Shape each ball into round flat naan bread.

7.On a baking sheet lined with parchment paper and place your naan bread dough and bake for 7 to 8 minutes and grill for 1 to 2 minutes from both sides in the oven until golden brown color develops on the top of flatbread naan.

8.Serve fresh and enjoy.

2.2 Tasty And Delicious Keto Gingerbread Cake

Total time of cooking

3 hours

Servings

16

Nutrition facts

Calories 287 (per slice)

Protein 9.3g

Net carbs 4.3g

Fat 26.4g

Ingredients:

Here is the list of ingredients required to make keto gingerbread cake.

- 3 cups of almond flour

- 1/2 cup of keto brown sugar

- 2 to 3 tablespoons of ginger

- 1 tablespoon of ground cinnamon

- 3 teaspoons of baking powder

- 1 teaspoon of baking soda

- 1 teaspoon of ground cloves

- 1 teaspoon of salt

- 1 teaspoon of ground nutmeg

- 6 eggs

- 300 ml of whipping cream

- 60 g of melted butter

- 1 cup of chopped walnuts

- 1/4 cup sugar-free maple syrup (optional)

Instructions:

Follow the method mentioned below to make keto gingerbread cake.

1.Assemble all the ingredients.

2. Into bread machine container add all the wet ingredients and on top add dry ingredients except walnuts. Select a simple setting for dough. At nut signal, add walnuts five minutes before the last kneading period completes.

3.Select the cake option from settings, choose the medium crust, and press start.

4.When baking finishes, remove the cake from the pan and let it cool down for a while.

5.Slice and sprinkle powdered sweetener on the top of the cake.

2.3 Easy Keto Sourdough Bread Rolls Recipe

Total time of cooking

2 hours

Servings

8

Nutrition facts

Calories 263 (per bread roll)

Protein 12g

Net carbs 2g

Fat 20g

Fiber 10g

Carbs 12g

Ingredients:

Here is the list of ingredients required to make keto sourdough bread rolls.

- 1 1/2 cups of almond flour

- 1/2 cup of coconut flour

- 1/2 cup of flax meal

- 1/2 cup of apple cider vinegar

- 1/3 cup of psyllium husk

- 3/4 cup of egg whites

- 3/4 cup of buttermilk

- 1/2 cup of warm water

- 1 scoop of keto unflavored whey protein

- 2 whole eggs

- 3 tablespoons of melted butter

- 2 teaspoon of instant yeast

- 1 teaspoon of Italian seasoning

- 1 teaspoon of kosher salt

Instructions:

Follow the method mentioned below to make keto sourdough bread rolls.

1. In your bread machine container, add all the ingredients and select dough cycle from your bread machine control panel, and press start.

2. Check Dough during kneading. Add water or flour if required according to the consistency of the Dough.

3. when the kneading cycle finished. Remove Dough from bread machine container.

4. Preheat oven at 350 f.

5.Line a baking sheet with parchment paper.

6.Divide Dough into eight pieces and make small loaves/rolls using your hands.

7.With a sharp knife, mark cuts on the top of each roll. Bake for 35 minutes or until each bread roll turned golden brown.

8.Then remove the baking sheet from the oven and brush the top of each bread roll with melted butter, and sprinkle Italian seasoning on the bread roll as well.

9.Place back again in the oven for 2 to 3 minutes under the grill until rolls turned deep golden brown from the top in color. (keep checking them during grill, so they

don't burn)

10.Serve fresh and enjoy.

2.4 Keto Fathead Cinnamon Rolls

Total time of cooking

1 hour 45 minutes

Servings

5

Nutrition facts

Calories 290 (per cinnamon roll)

Protein 13g

Net carbs 5g

Fat 24g

Fiber 4g

Carbs 9g

Ingredients:

Here is the list of ingredients required to make keto fathead cinnamon rolls.

- 1 3/4 cups of almond flour(superfine)

- 3/4 cup of mozzarella cheese

- 3 tablespoons of coconut flour

- 3 tablespoons of confectioners erythritol

- 4oz cream cheese

- 1 large egg

- 2 teaspoons of instant yeast

Ingredients for cinnamon roll filling:

- 3 tablespoons of granulated erythritol

- 1 tablespoon of cinnamon powder

- 1 tablespoon of melted butter

Ingredients for icing:

- 1/4 cup of erythritol

- 1 tablespoon of vanilla almond milk

Instructions:

Follow the method mentioned below to make fathead cinnamon rolls.

1.Assemble all the ingredients.

2.Microwave cream cheese and mozzarella cheese in the microwave-proof bowl until melted.

3.Put all the ingredients of a cinnamon roll dough, including melted cheese mixture, into the bread machine container(first liquids, then dry ingredients on the top). Select dough cycle and press the start button.

4..Once the dough cycle ends, remove the dough from the container and place it on a floured surface and knead it with your hands for few minutes.

5.Use your hands to work with dough. Press out dough into an oval shape, do not use a rolling pin; otherwise, the dough will stick to the pin.

6.Make sure your dough is about 1/4 inch thick and 16 inches long. Now coat the top of the dough first with the melted butter and sprinkle granulated erythritol and cinnamon powder all over the dough. Now roll up the dough and cut it into five equal-sized pieces.

7.Leave rolls for 20 minutes to let them rise a bit.

8.Grease Parchment paper-lined baking sheet with baking spray.

9.At 350 f degrees, bake for around 20 minutes or until golden brown.

10.Remove rolls from the oven and let them cool down for few minutes.

11.Make icing for rolls. Take a bowl and add confectioners erythritol and almond milk and mix until dissolved.

12.Coat cinnamon rolls with icing and enjoy.

2.5 Mini Crispy Crust Keto Quiche With Filling

Total time of cooking

1 hour 15 minutes

Servings

6

Nutrition facts

Calories 470 (per slice)

Protein 14.5g

Net carbs 5.5g

Fat 44.2g

Fiber 4.2g

Carbs 9.7g

Ingredients:

Here is the list of ingredients required to make keto quiche crust.

- 1/4 cup of Coconut flour

- 1/4 cup of almond flour

- 1/3 cup of cold butter

- 1 large egg

- 1/2 teaspoon of salt

Ingredients for egg mixture:

- 3/4 cup of whipping cream

- 4 large eggs

- 1/2 teaspoon of black pepper

- 1/2 teaspoon of salt

Ingredients for filling:

- Mozzarella cheese

- Smoked salmon

- Dill for garnishing

Instructions:

Follow the method mentioned below to make keto quiche crust.

1. Assemble all the ingredients of the crust.

2. Add all the ingredients mentioned above for quiche crust in the bread machine pan.

3. Close the lid, choose dough cycle, and press the start button.

4. When the kneading period ends, remove the dough, make a ball out of the dough with your hands. wrap the dough with foil, flatten it and freeze it for around 15 minutes.

5. Take out the dough from the freezer after 15 minutes and divide it into six equal portions.

6. Grease mini pie pan with butter.

7. Shape pie dough using your hands.

8. To avoid air bubbles, prick holes with a fork.

9. Again, freeze for 15 minutes.

10. After 15 minutes, bake for 15 to 16 mins at 350 f or 180 c if the dough's center rises during baking. Press down with the back of the spoon.

For egg mixture:

11. In a bowl, add all ingredients of the egg mixture mentioned above and whisk until well mixed.

Assembling:

12. Place cheese and smoked salmon into the baked crust.

13. Pour the egg mixture on top, garnish with dill.

14. Bake for 20 minutes at 350 f or 180 c.

2.6 Keto Garlic Bread

Total time of cooking

3 hours

Servings

12

Nutrition facts

Calories 309 (per slice)

Protein 9g

Net carbs 5.5g

Fat 29g

Carbs 5g

Ingredients:

Here is the list of ingredients required to make keto garlic bread.

- 2 1/2 cups of Almond flour

- 1 1/2 cups of egg whites

- 2/3 cup of melted butter

- 1 1/2 tablespoon bread machine yeast

- 1 teaspoon of salt

Ingredients for topping:

- 1/2 cup of melted butter

- 1 tablespoon of dried parsley

- 2 teaspoons of garlic powder

Instructions:

Follow the method mentioned below to make keto garlic bread.

1.Assemble all the ingredients of the crust.

2.Add all the garlic bread items to the bread machine container — liquid ingredients on the bottom and dry ingredients on top. Just be careful to keep the yeast away from the liquid by putting yeast on top of dry ingredients.

3.Select basic bread cycle and medium crust from the settings panel and press the start button.

4.When baking is finished, remove bread from the pan and let it cool completely on the oven rack.

5.Cut down into 12 equal pieces.

6.For the topping, in a boiler, mix together butter, parsley, and garlic powder.

7.Spread topping on the bread evenly.

8.Again, place in the oven and broil for few minutes to crisp up the bread.

9.Serve.

2.7 Keto Coconut Crust Pizza (Eggless)

Total time of cooking

1 hour

Servings

10

Nutrition facts

Calories 74 (per slice)

Protein 2.6g

Net carbs 0.8g

Fat 5.8g

Ingredients:

Here is the list of ingredients required to make keto coconut crust pizza.

- 1/2 cup of coconut flour

- 1/2 cup of grounded golden flaxseeds or flaxseed meal

- 2 tablespoons of olive oil

- 2 tablespoons of finely grounded psyllium husk

- 1 tablespoon of Italian seasoning

- 2 teaspoons of active dry yeast

- 1/2 teaspoon of salt

- 240 ml hot or boiling water

Ingredients for pizza sauce:

- 200g canned peeled tomatoes

- 2 to 3 tablespoons of tomatoes paste

- 2 tablespoons olive oil

- 2 to 3 teaspoons salt

- 1 teaspoon dry basil

- 1 teaspoon onion powder

- 1 teaspoon dried parsley

- 1 teaspoon garlic powder

- 1 teaspoon black pepper

- 1 teaspoon oregano

(Blend all the ingredients, until smooth paste/sauce is formed)

Ingredients for topping:

- 180g vegan cheese

- 3 to 4 sliced button mushrooms

- 4 to 5 sliced black olives

- tricolor capsicum (cut into strips)

- chopped parsley for garnishing

Instructions:

Follow the method mentioned below to make keto coconut crust pizza.

1. Assemble all the ingredients of the crust.

2. In bread machine container, add yeast and hot water together and mix and let it sit for 10 minutes, so the yeast dissolves in water and becomes creamy in texture.

3. After 10 minutes, add olive oil, coconut flour, flaxseeds, psyllium husk, Italian seasoning, and salt.

4. Close the lid: select dough cycle, and press the start button.

5. Remove dough from the bread machine. Spread out in greased pizza pan.

6. Cover with cloth or towel and set aside for around 25 minutes for rising.

7. Prick holes with a fork to release air bubbles during bake for around 15 to 20 minutes on the lowest rack of your oven at 350 f or 180 c, then flip over the side and bake for another 5 minutes.

8. Remove pizza from the oven, spread the pizza sauce, then add vegan cheese and all other ingredients mentioned in the topping list.

9. Bake again for 10 minutes on the middle rack of the oven.

10. Remove the pizza from the oven. When it's done, sprinkle chopped parsley all over the pizza.

11. Make slices with a pizza cutter and serve.

2.8 Tasty And Easy Keto Cornbread

Total time of cooking

1 hour 10 minutes

Servings

12

Nutrition facts

Calories 254 (per serving)

Protein 8.4g

Carbs 6g

Fat 22.7g

Fiber 3g

Ingredients:

Here is the list of ingredients required to make keto cornbread.

- 2 cups of almond flour

- 1 cup of shredded cheddar cheese

- 1/2 cup of melted butter

- 1/4 cup of coconut flour

- 1/4 cup of sour cream

- 2/3 can of baby corn roughly chopped

- 3 large eggs

- 2 1/2 teaspoons of instant yeast

- 1 teaspoon of pink Himalayan salt

- 25 drops of liquid stevia

Instructions:

Follow the method mentioned below to make keto coconut crust pizza.

1. Assemble all the ingredients of the crust.

2. In the bread machine pan, add all the ingredients except baby corn, starting with liquid ingredients first and dry ingredients in the last).close the lid and select dough cycle. Add water or flour if required during kneading.

3. When the machine beeps, five minutes before final kneading begins, add chopped baby corn.

4. Remove dough from the pan. Spread in a casserole dish.

5. Bake for around 40 to 42 minutes in the preheated oven at 350 f.

6. Allow to cool down for few minutes before slicing.

7. Serve and enjoy.

2.9 Keto Tomato And Parmesan buns

Total time of cooking

1 hour 40 minutes

Servings

5

Nutrition facts

Calories 261 (per bun)

Protein 14.5g

Net carbs 4.9g

Fat 18.9g

Fiber 8.3g

Ingredients:

Here is the list of ingredients required to make keto tomato and parmesan buns.

- 1/2 cup of coconut flour

- 3/4 cup of almond flour

- 1/4 cup flax meal

- 1/3 cup chopped sun-dried tomatoes

- 2/3 cup of parmesan cheese

- 2 1/2 tablespoons of psyllium husk powder

- 2 tablespoons of sesame seeds

- 2 teaspoon of active dry yeast

- 1 teaspoon cream of tartar

- 1/2 teaspoon of salt

- 1 cup boiling water

- 3 large egg whites

- 1 whole egg

Instructions:

Follow the method mentioned below to make keto tomato and parmesan buns.

1.Add all the ingredients in the bread machine container except sun-dried tomato. Start with liquid ingredients first, and then add all the dry ingredients with yeast on top. Make sure yeast does not come in contact with liquid.

2.Select dough from the control panel and start the machine.

3.Remove dough from the bread machine and divide into five equal parts. Make balls with the help of your hands.

4.Place them with a 2 to 3 inches gap (buns will grow in size once baked) on a non-stick Baking sheet .let it rise for around 25 minutes. Sprinkle sesame seeds all over the bun.

5.At 350 f in the preheated oven, bake for 35 to 40 minutes.

6.Remove once done and cool on a baking rack before serving.

2.10 Eggless Keto Focaccia

Total time of cooking

1 hour 45 minutes

Servings

25

Nutrition facts

Calories 105 (per serving)

Protein 2.1g

Net carbs 1.6g

Fat 8.9g

Ingredients:

Here is the list of ingredients required to make an eggless keto focaccia recipe

- 2 1/2 cups of almond flour

- 1/3 cup of golden flaxseeds

- 1/2 cup of coconut flour

- 2 cups of hot boiling water

- 5 tablespoons of psyllium husk powder

- 2 teaspoons of bread machine yeast

- 1 teaspoon of salt

For oil mixture:

- 1/2 cup of olive oil extra virgin

- 3 to 4 cloves garlic (minced)

- 1 teaspoon of dried or fresh thyme

- 1 teaspoon of dried or fresh thyme

- 1/2 teaspoon of black pepper

- 1/2 teaspoon of salt

Instructions:

Follow the method mentioned below to make eggless keto focaccia.

1.Turn on your stove and cook all the items mentioned in the list for oil mixture in a small pot over low to medium heat and until garlic turns brown, then turn off the stove. Keep two tablespoons of oil mixture for greasing the baking pan, two tablespoons to brush the dough's top, and remaining to add in the dough.

2.In the bread machine pan, add all the ingredients of focaccia mentioned in the list of ingredients above, including the remaining oil mixture. And start the dough cycle when the dough cycle ends. Remove the dough from the pan.

3.With two tablespoons of oil mixture, brush the bottom of a deep-dish pizza pan. Spread the dough into a pan, flatten the dough using your hands. make as many dimples as you like with your fingers on the dough.

4.With two tablespoons of the reserved oil, brush the top of the dough.

5.Sprinkle some flaky salt and some fresh thyme and rosemary on top(optional).

6.At 350 f preheated oven bake for about 30 to 40 minutes on lowest rack.

7.Turn off the oven once ready and for around 30 minutes, let it sit in the oven to dry.

8.Once completely cool, cut into small squares and enjoy.

2.11 Keto Fathead Dough Stuffed Sausage Buns

Total time of cooking

1 hour

Servings

6

Nutrition facts

Calories 363(per serving)

Protein 19g

fiber 1g

Carbs 3g

Fat 30g

Ingredients:

Here is the list of ingredients required to make keto fathead dough stuffed sausage buns.

For fathead dough:

- 1 oz of cream cheese

- 3/4 cup of almond flour

- 1.5 cup of mozzarella cheese

- 12 oz ground breakfast sausage(pre-seasoned)

- 1 large egg

- 1 1/2 teaspoons of instant yeast

Instructions:

Follow the method mentioned below to make keto fathead dough stuffed sausage buns.

1.Assemble all the ingredients.

2.Melt cream cheese and mozzarella cheese in the microwave for 30 seconds.

3.In the bread machine pan, add all the ingredients except sausages, choose dough cycle, and press start.

4.When the dough cycle completes, take out the dough from the bread machine pan.

5.Warm up your oven at 400 F.

6.Turn on the stove and preheat a pan to medium-high heat.

7.Cut pre-seasoned sausage into six pieces equally, add to the hot pan and cook. Once cooked, set aside and let them cool down.

8.Divide your dough into six equal balls. Use your hands to flatten out each ball or either roll it. Place cooked sausage in the middle of the dough, wrap it, and make a ball with your hands. Repeat the procedure with all other dough balls.

9.On a baking sheet lined with parchment paper, place sausage balls, put seam side down.

10.Bake for around 15 to 20 minutes or until golden browned.

11.Serve.

2.12 Keto Chicken Pot Pie Turnover bread

Total time of cooking

1 hour 15 minutes

Servings

9

Nutrition facts

Calories 589(per serving)

Protein 37.9g

Net carbs 9.6g

Fat 45.7g

Ingredients:

Here is the list of ingredients required to make keto chicken pot pie turnover bread.

Ingredients for dough:

- 3 cups of almond flour

- 7 cups of mozzarella cheese

- 2 eggs

- 1 tablespoon of water

- 2 teaspoon of xanthan gum

- 2 teaspoon of instant yeast

Ingredients for pot pie mixture:

- 1/2 cup of diced onion

- 3 cups of shredded cooked chicken

- 1/2 cup red onion diced

- 1 cup chicken broth

- 3 tablespoons of freshly chopped parsley

- 1 tablespoon of coconut flour

- 8 oz mushrooms chopped

- 4 oz cream cheese

- 1 teaspoon thyme

- 3 minced garlic cloves

Instructions:

Follow the method mentioned below to make keto chicken pot pie turnover bread.

1. Assemble all the ingredients.

2. Add all the ingredients of dough mentioned in the list in the bread machine pan, close the lid, choose dough cycle, and start the machine.

3. Take the dough out of the bread machine when kneading finishes. Cover with a kitchen towel for around 20 to 25 minutes and let it rise.

4. Turn on the stove over medium-high heat melt butter in a large pan.

5.Add onion and cook for five minutes until it softens. Now add mushrooms, garlic, and thyme, sprinkle pepper and salt and cook for 5 minutes more until mushroom becomes tender.

6.Add coconut flour, whisk in the broth and proceed to cook for 3 to 5 minutes until the mixture thickens. Add chicken and turn the heat to low.

7.Add cream cheese and cook until cream cheese is fully melted. Add parsley and sprinkle salt. Remove from the stove and turn off the heat, and let it cool down.

8.To ensure all ingredients are fully combined, knead the dough with your hands.

9.Lay down parchment paper on a floured surface, place dough over it, put another parchment paper on top, and roll dough with a rolling pin into a rectangular shape (dough should be around 1/4 inches thick). Cut edges of the dough to form a perfect rectangular shape using a knife or pizza cutter. Cut further into nine tiny rectangles.

10.Place a spoonful of chicken pot pie mixture into each rectangle and fold over. Repeat the same procedure with other rectangles.

11.With egg brush, the tops of turnover bread.

12.Place turnovers in a non-stick baking sheet and bake for 20 minutes at 375 f degrees.

13.Serve and enjoy.

2.13 Keto Pecan Chocolate Pie

Total time of cooking

2 hour 15 minutes

Servings

8

Nutrition facts

Calories 504(per serving)

Protein 11g

Carbs 11g

Fat 49g

Fiber 7g

Ingredients:

Here is the list of ingredients required to make keto pecan chocolate pie.

For the sweet pie crust:

- 1.25 cups of almond flour

- 1/4 cup of cream cheese

- 3 tablespoons of unsalted butter

- 2 tablespoons of coconut flour

- 1 beaten egg

- 1/2 teaspoon of xanthan gum

- 1 teaspoon of instant yeast

- 1/4 pink Himalayan salt

- 15 drops of stevia

For the chocolate pie filling:

- 1 cup of heavy whipping cream

- 1 cup of raw chopped pecans

- 1/4 cup of butter

- 3 eggs large (room temperature)

- 4 oz unsweetened chocolate chopped

- 2 tablespoons of erythritol

- 1 teaspoon of vanilla extract

- 1/4 teaspoon of pink salt

- 1/4 teaspoon liquid stevia

Instructions:

Follow the method mentioned below to make keto chocolate pie.

1. Add all the sweet pie crust ingredients to the bread machine container. Select the dough cycle press the start button.

2. When kneading completes, remove dough from pan, make a ball of dough seal in plastic wrap, and freeze for at least 20 minutes.

3. Take out the dough after 20 minutes from the freezer. Place dough between two parchment papers, roll out the dough using a rolling pin, spread on the greased pie pan, flatten dough with your fingers, and prick holes using a fork in the crust.

4. Freeze again for 15 minutes.

5. At 350 F/180 C preheated oven, bake for 15 minutes or until it turns light brown.

6. Once done, allow the crust to cool down. Meanwhile, make the chocolate pie filling.

7. On a double boiler, heat butter, and heavy cream until it completely melts down, remove from the boiler and add the chocolate mix well until it turns smooth in texture. Add vanilla extract, erythritol, stevia, and salt and mix well until dissolved.

8.In a separate bowl, whisk eggs, add them into the chocolate mixture, and mix until completely blends.

9.Spread pecans on the bottom layer of cooled pie. Then pour the chocolate mixture on top and bake again for 20 minutes.

10.Before serving, let the tart cool for a while.

11. Before eating, sprinkle with unsweetened cocoa powder or powdered erythritol.

2.14 Starbucks Inspired Keto Poppy Seeds And Lemon Loaf

Total time of cooking

3 hour 40 minutes

Servings

12

Nutrition facts

Calories 201(per serving)

Protein 9g

Carbs 6g

Fat 17g

Fiber 3g

Ingredients:

Here is the list of ingredients required to make poppy seeds and lemon loaf.

- 2 1/8 cups of almond flour

- 1/2 cup of any sweetener

- 6 eggs large

- 3 tablespoons of unsalted melted butter

- 2 tablespoons of poppy seeds

- 2 tablespoons of lemon juice

- 1 1/2 heaping tablespoons of lemon zest

- 1 1/2 bread machine yeast

For Glaze:

- 1/2 cup of erythritol(powdered)

- 1 to 2 tablespoons of water

- 1 tablespoon of lemon juice

Instructions:

Follow the method mentioned below to make poppy seeds and lemon bread.

1.Combine all the ingredients in the bread machine container in the order suggested by your bread maker.

2.Pick basic bread and medium crust from the options of the bread machine control panel. And press the start button.

3.Check during kneading. Add two tablespoons of water if needed.

4.When baking finishes, remove bread from the bread machine container.

5.Leave it for 15 minutes to cool down before slicing.

6.For Glaze add lemon juice and erythritol to a bowl and slowly add water mix until fully incorporated.

7.Spread the Glaze over cooled bread slices and enjoy.

Chapter 3: Bread Machine Dinner Recipes

3.1 Keto Garlic Flatbread

Total time of cooking

1 hour 20 minutes

Servings

8

Nutrition facts

Calories 134(per serving)

Protein 7.7g

Net carbs 2.1g

Fat 9.9g

Ingredients:

Here is the list of ingredients required to make keto garlic flatbread.

Ingredients for dough:

- 1/2 cup of grated mozzarella cheese

- 1/2 cup of ground almonds or milled linseed

- 1 cup of courgette grated

- 1/3 cup of coconut flour

- 3 large eggs

- 1 1/2 teaspoons of bread machine yeast

- 1 teaspoon of garlic powder

- 1 teaspoon of mixed herbs

- 1 teaspoon of baking powder

- 1/4 teaspoon of xanthan gum

- 1/4 teaspoon of salt

For the garlic butter:

- 2 tablespoons of butter melted

- 1 to 2 garlic cloves (minced)

Instructions:

Follow the method mentioned below to make keto garlic flatbread.

1.Assemble all the ingredients.

2.Place keto garlic flatbread ingredients in the bread machine container, choose dough cycle, and start the machine. After five minutes of kneading, check the dough's consistency add one to two tablespoons of water if required.

3.Take out the dough from the bread machine once the dough cycle finishes. Grease your non-stick round pizza pan and spread the dough. Flatten the dough using your hands. leave it for 10 minutes to rise.

4.Place the baking pan in 350 degrees preheated oven and bake for around 25 to 30 minutes or until flatbread turns light golden brown.

5.Turn on your stove at low, medium heat. In a pan, heat butter first, then add minced garlic and cook until garlic turns nut brown.

6.Spread garlic butter mixture over the top of flatbread and brush evenly all over the baked flatbread.

7.Cut flatbread into eight slices and serve.

3.2 Simple And Tasty Keto Zucchini Bread

Total time of cooking

3 hours 20 minutes

Servings

14

Nutrition facts

Calories 186(per serving)

Protein 8.3g

Net carbs 2.7g

Fat 15.1g

Ingredients:

Here is the list of ingredients required to make keto zucchini bread.

- 1 1/2 cups of grated zucchini(courgette)

- 1/2 cup of ground almonds

- 3/4 cup of melted unsalted butter

- 2/3 cup of grated mozzarella cheese

- 2/3 cup of coconut flour

- 5 eggs large

- 2 teaspoons of bread machine yeast

- 1 teaspoon of dried oregano

- 1/2 teaspoon of xanthan gum

- 1/2 teaspoon of salt

Instructions:

Follow the method mentioned below to make keto zucchini bread.

1.Assemble all the ingredients.

2.Remove the Bread machine container. Add all the ingredients of zucchini keto bread to the container. Place the container into the bread machine, close the lid, select basic bread cycle and medium crust, and press the start button.

3.Check the dough consistency. After five minutes, add two tablespoons of water if required.

4.When the Baking period is finished. Remove the bread from the pan and place it into the cooling rack for some time.

5.Cut into slices and serve.

3.3 Low Carb Keto Pumpkin Spice Bread

Total time of cooking

3 hours

Servings

12

Nutrition facts

Calories 191(per serving)

Protein 7g

Net carbs 4g

Fat 16g

Total carbs 7g

Ingredients:

Here is the list of ingredients required to make pumpkin bread.

- 2 cups of almond flour

- 3/4 cup pumpkin puree

- 3/4 cup of erythritol

- 5 medium-sized eggs

- 4 tablespoons of softened butter

- 3 tablespoons of heavy whipping cream

- 2 tablespoons of coconut flour

- 3 teaspoons of pumpkin pie spice

- 1 1/2 teaspoons of instant yeast

- 1 teaspoon vanilla extract

Instructions:

Follow the method mentioned below to make keto pumpkin bread.

1.In a Bread machine container, add all the ingredients(liquids first followed by the dry ingredients in the end).

2.Select basic bread settings, medium crust, and loaf size. Start the machine.

3.After 5 minutes of mixing check dough, add 2 to 3 tablespoons of water required.

4.Once baking is done. Shift bread to a cooling rack and let it cool down completely.

5.Cut into 12 equal slices and serve.

3.4 Tasty And Easy Keto Olive Bread

Total time of cooking

2 hours

Servings

16

Nutrition facts

Calories 93(per serving)

Protein 3.5g

Net carbs 1.7g

Fat 6.4g

Ingredients:

Here is the list of ingredients required to make keto olive bread.

- 1 cup of hot water

- 3/4 cup of coconut flour

- 3 whole eggs

- 3/4 cup of golden flaxseed

- 3/4 cup of black olives(cut in small cubes)

- 3 tablespoons of psyllium husk (finely grounded)

- 3 tablespoons of apple cider vinegar

- 2 tablespoons of olive oil

- 2 teaspoons of instant yeast

- 1 teaspoon of salt

- 1 teaspoon of basil

- 1 teaspoon of ground oregano

- 1 teaspoon of thyme

- 1/2 teaspoon of garlic powder

Instructions:

Follow the method mentioned below to make keto olive bread.

1.Follow the order recommended by your bread maker, except olives add all the ingredients to the pan.

2.Choose your bread maker dough settings.

3.Five minutes before the last kneading cycle when the machine beeps, add olives

4.when the dough is formed, remove it from the bread machine.

5.Spread the dough evenly in the loaf pan lined with parchment paper.

6.Bake at 350 f at the middle rack of the preheated oven for 40 minutes .

7.Cooldown for sometime before slicing.

3.5 Classic Keto Meatloaf Recipe

Total time of cooking

2 hours 30 minutes

Servings

14

Nutrition facts

Calories 245(per serving)

Protein 13g

Net carbs 2g

Fat 19g

fiber 1g

Ingredients:

Here is the list of ingredients required to make keto meatloaf.

For meatloaf:

- 2 lbs ground beef

- 1 cup of almond flour

- 2 eggs large

- 1/2 chopped onion

- 4 garlic cloves (minced)

- 1 teaspoon of salt

- 1 teaspoon instant yeast

- 1/4 teaspoon of black pepper

For meatloaf sauce:

- 1/2 of cup tomato sauce (sugar-free)

- 2 tablespoons of mustard

- 2 tablespoons of vinegar

- 2 tablespoons of sweetener

- 2 tablespoons of olive oil

- 2 tablespoons of Worcestershire sauce

Instructions:

Follow the method mentioned below to make keto meatloaf.

1.Assemble all the ingredients.

2.In the bread machine container, add the eggs, almond flour, ground beef, garlic cloves, onion, black, salt, and instant yeast. Close the lid and select the dough option from the bread machine control panel.

2.During kneading, check the dough's consistency if required, add 2 to 3 tablespoons of water.

3.Turn off the bread machine once the dough cycle completes. Transfer the loaf mixture to a non-stick loaf pan.

4.Bake at 350 F/180 C for 35 minutes in the preheated oven.

5.Add all the ingredients in a medium mixing bowl mentioned in the list for meatloaf sauce. mix until combine .

6.Spread sauce evenly over top of the meatloaf. And bake for 40 minutes more.

7.Let it cool down for 15 minutes before serving.

3.6 Classic Keto Cheese Bread

Total time of cooking

4 hours

Servings

16

Nutrition facts

Calories 88(per serving)

Protein 3.25g

Carbs 2.25g

Fat 7.5g

fiber 0.3g

Ingredients:

Here is the list of ingredients required to make keto classic cheese bread.

- 1/4 cup of melted butter

- 1/2 cup of peanut flour

- 4 large egg yolks

- 5 oz cream cheese

- 2 tablespoons of golden monk fruit sweetener

- 1 teaspoon bread machine yeast

- 1 teaspoon Himalayan salt

- 1 teaspoon vanilla extract

Instructions:

Follow the method mentioned below to make keto classic cheese bread.

1.In order suggested by your bread maker. Add all the ingredients into the bread machine container (liquid ingredients first, then dry ingredients).

2.Choose basic bread settings and light crust also loaf size.

3.Start the machine check the dough during the kneading period. If needed, add two to three tablespoons of water.

4.Once baking is finished. Turn off the machine and let bread rest for few minutes.

5.Place bread on a cooling rack and leave it for 10 to 15 minutes.

6.Cut into 16 slices and enjoy.

3.7 Easy Keto Dinner Buns Low Carb

Total time of cooking

1 hour 50 minutes

Servings

8

Nutrition facts

Calories 170(per serving)

Protein 7g

Net Carbs 2g

Fat 13g

Ingredients:

Here is the list of ingredients required to make keto dinner buns.

- 1 1/4 cups of almond flour

- 1 cup of hot water

- 3 egg whites

- 5 tablespoons of psyllium husk powder

- 2 tablespoons of sesame seeds

- 2 teaspoons of bread machine yeast

- 2 teaspoons of vinegar

- 1/2 teaspoon of rock salt

Instructions:

Follow the method mentioned below to make keto dinner buns.

1.In order suggested by your bread maker. Add water, vinegar, egg whites, almond flour, psyllium husk powder, rock salt, and yeast(liquid ingredients first, then dry ingredients).

2.Choose dough cycle and start the machine.

3.Take out the dough from the pan once the dough cycle ends.

4.Divide dough into eight equal portions. And make balls with your hands. to prevent dough from sticking your hands, wet your hands a little before doing this.

5.Leave them for around 20 minutes to let them rise in size.

6.Place buns in a parchment paper-lined baking sheet with a 2 to 3 inches gap.

7.On top of each bun, sprinkle white and black sesame seeds.

8.Put in the oven preheated oven for 50 to 55 minutes at 350 F/ 180 C.

9.Let it cool down before eating.

3.8 Delicious And Easy Keto Tahini Almond Bread

Total time of cooking

2 hour 50 minutes

Servings

10

Nutrition facts

Calories 160(per serving)

Protein 7.3g

Carbs 0.6g

Fat 13.5g

Ingredients:

Here is the list of ingredients required to make tahini bread.

- 1 cup of tahini

- 1/2 cup of almond flour

- 2 large size eggs

- 1 1/2 tablespoons of lemon juice

- 2 teaspoons of chia seeds

- 1 teaspoon of vanilla extract

- 1 teaspoon of instant yeast

- 1 teaspoon of salt

Instructions:

Follow the method mentioned below to make tahini almond bread.

1. Add eggs, lemon juice, vanilla extract, tahini, almond flour, chia seeds, yeast, and salt into your bread machine container.

2.Close the bread machine's lid, pick the basic bread settings and medium crust, press the start button.

3.Once the bread is baked, let it rest few minutes in the bread machine.

4.Remove the bread from bread machine and transfer to oven rack for cooling purpose.

5.Once the bread is cooled down, slice and serve.

3.9 Keto Low Carb Savory Pie-Salmon Quiche

Total time of cooking

2 hour 20 minutes

Servings

10

Nutrition facts

Calories 320.42(per serving)

Protein 15.95g

Total Carbs 6.98g

Fat 25.54g

Fiber 3.02g

Sugar 1.4g

Ingredients:

Here is the list of ingredients required to make keto low-carb savory pie.

For the savory pie crust:

- 3/4 cup of almond flour

- 3 tablespoons of coconut flour

- 1/3 cup of sesame seeds

- 3 tablespoons of olive oil

- 3 to 4 tablespoons of water

- 1 egg large

- 2 teaspoons of instant yeast

- 1/2 teaspoon of salt

For quiche filling:

- 8 oz salmon

- 1/2 cup of whipping cream

- 1/2 cup of shredded cheese

- 1/4 cup of parmesan

- 4 eggs

- 1 chopped small onion

- 1 chopped green onion

- 2 1/2 tablespoons of butter

- 1 1/2 tablespoons of fresh dill or parsley

- 1/4 teaspoon ground black pepper

- 1 teaspoon salt

Instructions:

Follow the method mentioned below to make keto low-carb savory pie.

1. Add all the savory pie crust ingredients to the bread machine container. Select the dough cycle press the start button.

2. When kneading completes, remove dough and spread on the greased pie pan, flatten dough with your fingers and prick holes using a fork in the crust.

3. At 350 F/180 C preheated oven, bake for 15 minutes or until it turns light brown.

4. Once done, allow the crust to cool down. Meanwhile, make salmon quiche filling.

5. On a medium heat pan, sauté onion in butter until it softens.

6. In a separate bowl, add eggs, whipping cream, cheese, pepper, and salt, whisk until well mixed.

7.On baked crust, first spread cooked onion and fresh parsley/dill, .then add salmon and egg mixture on top.

8.Bake again for 35 to 40 minutes.

9.Allow the salmon quiche to cool for 10 minutes before serving.

10.Serve with fresh cream or salad.

3.10 Keto Fathead Stuffed Pizza Buns

Total time of cooking

1 hour 30 minutes

Servings

4

Nutrition facts

Calories 443(per serving)

Protein 26g

Total Carbs 10g

Fat 34g

Fiber 2g

Ingredients:

Here is the list of ingredients required to make keto fathead stuffed pizza buns.

For fathead dough:

- 1 1/2 cups of shredded mozzarella (melted)

- 3 eggs (1 for egg wash,2 for dough)

- 3/4 cup of almond flour

- 5 tablespoons of cream cheese (melted)

- 2 teaspoons of instant yeast

- 2 teaspoons of xanthan gum

- pinch of salt

For the stuffed filling:

- 1/4 cup cheddar or mozzarella cheese

- 4 tablespoons of cooked Italian sausage

- 8 slices of pepperoni

- 2 tablespoons of feta cheese

For garnishing:

- 1/4 cup of shredded parmesan

- 1 tablespoon of butter

- 1 teaspoon of Italian seasoning

Instructions:

Follow the method mentioned below to make keto fathead pizza buns.

1.Assemble all the ingredients.

2.In the bread machine container, add all the ingredients of fathead pizza dough in the order suggested by your bread machine: select dough cycle and press start. During kneading, checks dough consistency if required, add two tablespoons of water.

3.When the machine beeps, remove dough from the pan and knead with wet hands for few minutes. Divide the dough into four equal balls.

4.Flatten all four dough balls with a rolling pin, fill in the stuffed filling ingredients in the center of each ball and close the ball with your hands.

5.Brush each ball with egg wash, place stuffed pizza buns on a non-stick baking sheet and bake for 25 to 30 minutes on the middle rack of the oven at 350 F/180 C.

6.Mix Italian seasoning with melted butter and brush over the top of each bun. Sprinkle parmesan cheese over the pizza buns and serve.

3.11 Keto Onion And Cheese Bread Low Carb

Total time of cooking

3 hour 10 minutes

Servings

23

Nutrition facts

Calories 75(per serving)

Protein 7.5g

Net Carbs 1.5g

Fat 7g

Fiber 1g

Ingredients:

Here is the list of ingredients required to make keto onion and cheese bread.

- 2 cups of almond flour

- 1.5 cups of shredded cheese

- 1/4 cup of chopped green onions

- 1 cup of water

- 1/4 cup of sour cream

- 1/2 chopped small onion

- 4 scoops of unflavored whey powder

- 1 chopped shallot

- 3 minced garlic cloves

- 2 teaspoon of instant yeast

- 1 teaspoon of chili flakes

- 1 teaspoon of xanthan gum

- 1/2 teaspoon of salt

- 1/2 teaspoon of pepper

Instructions:

Follow the method mentioned below to make keto onion and cheese bread.

1.Put all the onion and cheese bread ingredients into the bread machine pan in the order suggested by your bread maker. Do not add onions and shallot Close down the lid of the machine, select simple bread settings and choose medium crust, and start the machine.

2.When the machine beeps for extra ingredients, add onions and shallot.

3.When done, remove baked bread from the pan and let it cool down.

4.Once cooled, cut into slices and enjoy.

3.12 Keto Pesto Chicken Cheese Pizza

Total time of cooking

1 hour

Servings

8

Nutrition facts

Calories 387(per slice)

Protein 27.2g

Net Carbs 5.1g

Fat 28.9g

Ingredients:

Here is the list of ingredients required to make keto pesto chicken cheese pizza.

- 1 1/2 cups of almond flour

- 1 egg

- 3 1/2 cups of shredded mozzarella

- 2 tablespoons of olive oil

- 2 to 3 tablespoons of water

- 1 1/2 teaspoons of dry yeast

- 1 teaspoon of xanthan gum

- 1 teaspoon of salt

For topping:

- 3/4 cup of shredded chicken

- 1/2 cups of shredded mozzarella

- 6 cherry tomatoes

- 3 tablespoons of pesto

- 2 tablespoons of sliced roasted bell pepper

- 1 1/2 tablespoons of keto garlic sauce

- 4 oz sliced mozzarella

Instructions:

Follow the method mentioned below to make keto pesto chicken cheese pizza.

1.Meltdown 3 1/2 cups of mozzarella cheese in a microwave oven.

2.Place water, olive oil, egg, mozzarella cheese, almond flour, xanthan gum, salt, and yeast on top of dry ingredients into the machine pan.

3.Pick dough cycle from settings and start the machine.

4.When the kneading procedure is done, remove it from the machine, roll it out with a rolling pin, and spread it into greased pizza sheet.

5.Cover the pizza pan and leave it for 25 minutes to rise.

6.Spread pesto and garlic sauce evenly on the top of the pizza crust.

7.Top up with chicken, tomatoes, bell pepper, shredded cheese, and sliced mozzarella.

8.Bake for 20 minutes at 380 F preheated oven until the crust turns golden brown, and cheese melts down.

9.Make eight slices with a pizza cutter and serve.

3.13 Classic Keto Baguette With Garlic Butter

Total time of cooking

1 hour 50 minutes

Servings

32

Nutrition facts

Calories 27(For 2 baguettes, per serving)

Protein 1.2g

Net Carbs 0.4g

Total Fat 1.4g

Ingredients:

Here is the list of ingredients required to make a classic keto baguette with garlic butter.

For Baguettes dough:

- 1 cup hot water

- 3/4 cup of coconut flour

- 3/4 cup of golden flaxseed (make a powder using seeds grinder)

- 6 large egg whites

- 3 tablespoons of apple cider vinegar

- 3 tablespoons of psyllium husk

- 2 teaspoons of instant yeast

- 1/2 teaspoon of salt

For the garlic butter:

- 1/2 cup of softened butter

- 1/4 cup of any cheese of your choice

- 4 tablespoons of minced garlic

- 1 1/2 teaspoon of parsley

(Mix them all in a bowl)

Instructions:

Follow the method mentioned below to make a keto baguette.

1.Gather all the ingredients.

2.Place all the ingredients for the baguette in the bread machine container, start the machine and choose the dough cycle.

3.Once done, place your dough into a floured surface and knead for few minutes, divide into two portions and make two 9" inches long dough.

4.On the baking sheet, place both doughs. Mark diagonal cuts on the top of the dough.

5.For about 45 to 50 minutes, bake at 350 F/180 C preheated oven.

6.Place baguettes on the wire rack for cooling.

7.Cut each baguette into slices and spread garlic bread before serving.

8.Enjoy

3.14 Tasty Cheese And Garlic Pull-Apart Keto Bread

Total time of cooking

1 hour 25 minutes

Servings

10

Nutrition facts

Calories 302(per serving)

Protein 16g

Carbs 6g

Fat 10g

Fiber 3g

Ingredients:

Here is the list of ingredients required to make cheese and garlic pull-apart bread.

- 1 1/3 cups of almond flour

- 3 cups of grated mozzarella cheese

- 1 cup of grated cheddar cheese

- 1/4 cups of sliced green onion

- 2 medium-sized eggs

- 2 garlic cloves

- 4 tablespoons of salted butter

- 2 tablespoons of warm water

- 2 tablespoons of chives

- 2 teaspoons of dried yeast

- 2 teaspoons of inulin

- 2 teaspoons of xanthan gum

- 1 teaspoon of salt

- pinch of pepper

Instructions:

Follow the method mentioned below to make cheese and garlic pull-apart bread.

1.In a microwave-safe bowl, mix cheese and butter until completely melts.

2.Combine inulin, yeast, and warm water in a bread machine container, leave it for 15 to 20 minutes and let it proof.

3.Now, on top of the yeast mixture, add almond flour, salt, xanthan gum, pour eggs followed by melted cheese and butter mixture, choose dough cycle and start the machine.

4.Once kneading is over. Transfer the dough into a bowl and cover with a kitchen cloth to rise for 20 minutes.

5.Knead the dough with hands for a while, roll out into a rectangular shape on the floured surface.

6.Spread over the cheddar, cheese, garlic, green onions, chive, salt, and pepper.

7.Make a large scroll , rolling the dough from one end to the other.

8.Slit the dough at an angle(approx 3/4 of the way through) with kitchen scissors. Twist each portion of the dough oppositely from the previous one. To overlap the portions and form more of an oval shape. Press the dough together.

9.Place at the greased non-stick baking sheet and leave for 20 minutes.

10.Bake your pull-apart bread for 25 to 30 minutes at 350 F/180 C preheated oven.

11.Allow cooling first for 10 to 15 minutes.

12.Serve on a platter and enjoy.

3.15 Low Carb Keto Spinach Bread

Total time of cooking

3 hour 5 minutes

Servings

8

Nutrition facts

Calories 345(per serving)

Protein 13g

Carbs 7g

Fat 31g

Fiber 4g

Ingredients:

Here is the list of ingredients required to make spinach bread.

- 1 3/4 cups of almond flour

- 1 cup of cheddar cheese

- 1 cup of spinach finely chopped

- 2 eggs large

- 7 tablespoons of melted butter

- 1 tablespoon of rosemary chopped

- 2 clove of garlic finely chopped

- 2 teaspoons of instant yeast

- 1/2 teaspoon of salt

Instructions:

Follow the method mentioned below to make spinach bread.

1. Combine all the ingredients.

2. Put all the ingredients except spinach into your bread maker in the order recommended by your bread machine.

3. Pick bread cycle and medium crust from your bread maker settings panel and start the machine.

4. Check after 5 minutes of kneading. Add two tablespoons of water if needed.

5. At nut signals, add spinach to the mixture.

6.When the bread cycle completes, Remove and allow to cool down for a while.

7.Slice and serve.

3.16 Keto Mexican Jalapeno Cornbread

Total time of cooking

1 hour 15 minutes

Servings

8

Nutrition facts

Calories 412(per serving)

Protein 13g

Carbs 6g

Fat 40g

Fiber 3g

Ingredients:

Here is the list of ingredients for Mexican jalapeno cornbread.

- 2 cups of almond flour

- 1 cup of grated cheddar cheese

- 1 cup of heavy cream

- 1/4 cup of melted butter

- 4 large beaten eggs

- 3 tablespoons of diced jalapenos

- 1 teaspoon of instant yeast

- 1/2 teaspoon of salt

Instructions:

Follow the method mentioned below to make Mexican jalapeno cornbread.

1. Assemble all the ingredients.

2. In the bread maker pan, add all the ingredients except jalapenos, select dough cycle, and start the machine. Check after few minutes if needed, add two tablespoons of water.

3. When the machine beeps five minutes before the last kneading, add jalapenos.

4. Warm up your oven at 350 F.

5. Spray 8 inches oven-safe iron skillet.

6. Place your dough batter into an iron skillet and bake for around 30 minutes.

7. Remove from oven once done, cut in 8 slices, and serve.

Conclusion

The bread machine is such a blessing in the shape of an appliance to get your hands on. The more you play with it and bake new things, the more you can create magic with it and never want to get away with the feeling of how it saves your time and energy and why you always want one in your kitchen.

Practice makes things perfect, so do not hesitate to experiment. You may not master the art of making bread and using a bread machine in just one day. However, you can kick start your learning journey with ample bread recipes combined in this cookbook. Regardless of your expertise in making different kinds of bread and operating a bread machine. Buying and starting with a cookbook will reveal a world of new recipes to you.

Keto Bread and Keto Snacks

Keto Flex Academy

Table of Contents

Introduction

With the constant influx of foods and snacks around us all day, it might be really hard to stick to a diet. This means that your diet must always incorporate foods and snacks that you actually enjoy so that you aren't tempted into eating things that will break your diet and hinder your progress. Usually, a snack on a diet would mean a few pieces of steamed broccoli or a handful of green beans, however, those things don't exactly get our mouths watering, do they?

No, they definitely don't. We all surely crave a muffin or two or a big chocolate chip cookie with some tea. However, most of the time, these items will include ingredients that are prohibited in the diets we're trying to follow.

This is where this book will surely come in handy. With a large variety of recipes for bread and other snacks that incorporate the ketogenic diet in an easy and delicious way, it also will provide you with tips and methods to make sure you're able to follow and maintain the diet. It will then include essential ingredients, their nutritional value as well as information on the baking tools and skills you will need. The recipes will include easy-to-make bread and snacks, incorporate plant-based recipes, as well as pre- and post- workout bites to keep you satisfied all while following the Keto diet.

The keto diet is undoubtedly a healthy lifestyle choice and it surely has many beneficial aspects to your life and wellbeing. This book aims to make sure you can maintain it by providing you with recipes to brighten up your diet and help you enjoy your meals all while keeping your keto regime intact.

Part 1 - Keto Bread and Keto Snacks Essentials

Chapter 1: The Keto Diet

The Ketogenic diet, popularly trending as the 'keto diet' is a diet where your objective is to eat as little carbohydrates as possible and as much fat as you like. Now, even though we dread carbs and know what a damning effect it has on our waistlines, it's a vital component of the body's natural functionality. Our bodies use carbs in the form of glucose for energy, it's as simple as that. When you so drastically reduce the amount of carbs your body is given, it goes into a state called **ketosis**. This state is when your body looks to all its stored fat and produces ketone bodies out of them. These ketone bodies then act as the energy source your body needs to function and takes the place of the carbs that would usually do that. You may be skeptical at first, thinking how your body could manage to do that for itself, but it's a natural instinct and has been occurring since the beginning of time. Many animals use ketosis to survive long periods without a sufficient energy source and if that isn't convincing enough, the benefits are sure to be what sells.

A number of studies[1] have shown the numerous benefits of the keto diet, from weight loss, lowered insulin and cholesterol levels to prevention and treatment of diabetes and even cancer! It really is no wonder why it has gained so much recognition and praise over the last few years.

The method of going about this diet is like any other. It requires determination and sacrifice. You have to stop eating all those carb-laden dishes you love and opt for healthier options. Once you're able to do that, your body will respond accordingly and you will start to reap the benefits.

Here's how you can start and maintain[2] the Keto diet to ensure you're one of the lucky ones who reap all of the wondrous benefits:

1. Do some digging

Before you start a diet, the first thing you need to do is find out everything you possibly can about it. This includes the right way to do it, its benefits as well as health risks, and all the sacrifices you are going to have to make. Most of the time, the best thing to do before starting a diet is to find out from your doctor whether you actually can do it. More often than not, people find themselves in bad situations when they decide to do it themselves without seeking out medical advice. Another thing is to make sure you're ready to do it - this means you need to set a goal, prepare for it, and keep following through until you reach the desired outcome. When you plan and keep yourself in the know about the diet, like current research and adjustments and improvements, you'll be giving yourself the best chance to progress.

2. Lower your carbs and maximize your healthy fats and proteins

Once you've decided to do the keto diet, make sure you do it right. This means limiting the number of carbs you eat on a daily basis, ensuring you eat as many healthy fats as

---

[1] (Mawer, 2018)
[2] (Spritzler, 2016)

possible, and also making sure that you get enough protein and fiber into your diet as well. To ensure you follow through with these restrictions, you're going to have to invest in new food items and new ways of cooking and eating and so this is something you should be prepared for if you are a fussy eater.

3. Exercise!

Doing exercise whilst on the keto diet can help you reach ketosis faster. This is because when you exercise, you deplete all of your glycogen stores and this means that you will have to stock up on them again when you consume carbs. On the keto diet, however, you eat little to no carbs at all, and this means your body naturally goes into ketosis to try and make its own sources of energy. This means that when you exercise, you're basically speeding up that process.

4. Pair it with fasting

Another way to accelerate your ketosis is to fast. Fasting is very often paired with the keto diet because it once again limits the amount of food you're taking in. This means your body isn't getting the energy it needs to function and so its backup system kicks in and pushes you into ketosis.

5. Make adjustments

Not all people can fast or diet or maintain an extremely strict no-carb diet from the very start. It takes time and energy to get it right for you specifically. Do not expect too many results too soon as it is a process that takes a few weeks to kick in. When something isn't working for you, make changes. If you feel you cannot stay away from foods that you are used to, supplement them with foods that are healthier and will still satisfy you. It is all about making changes and ensuring that you are able to find a balance that works for you.

Chapter 2: Ingredients, Baking Skills, and Tools

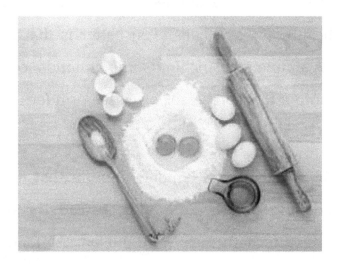

Ingredients and their Nutritional Value

Flour

Now, when we see the term "bread" it automatically rings some alarm bells. Firstly, bread is known to be one of the main sources of carbs for most people and secondly, most bread will always contain a high flour content. Normal flour made out of wheat is a very complex carbohydrate because of how much it has been processed. What this means for a keto diet is that almost any type of food that would usually contain flour is almost always restricted. We're lucky though - because modern technology and innovative thinking have produced low carb flour alternatives. These alternatives are really important if you want your keto diet foods to be fun and familiar without all the added carbohydrate content.

One of the first ingredients a keto dieter should become familiar with is the different variants of **flour:**

- **Almond Flour and Almond Meal**

Almond flour is extremely versatile in the baking process because of its gluten-free property as well as its lovely almond nut flavor. It is simply made by grinding up blanched (skinless) almonds into a powder. Almond flour is most often used as a direct substitute for regular wheat powder and thus can be used in almost all recipes. With the rise in popularity of the keto diet and the need for a flour substitute, it is available at almost all grocery or health stores. What's even better is that if you wish to make it yourself, you can! It's as simple as blanching some almonds, completely drying them, and then putting them into a food processor or coffee grinder until they become a fine powder.

Almond meal is slightly different than almond flour in that its consistency is a little grainier. It also isn't made with blanched almonds, instead, the almonds are ground up into a slightly crumbly texture with their skin still on. Almond meal can be used to achieve a crunchier texture in foods and is typically used in crusts and bases.

It typically includes 4 grams of carbs, 50 grams of fat, 20 grams of protein, and 10 grams of fiber which all equate to around 600 calories per 100 grams

- **Coconut Flour**

Not only is it highly nutritional with high amounts of fiber, protein, as well as healthy fats, but it also tastes delicious. It also has a low amount of carbs which makes it ideal for the keto diet. It is made from the meat of the coconut and it is usually a by-product of coconut milk because the meat is blended with water and then drained, where the liquid becomes the milk. The leftover meat is then put into an oven to be dehydrated and slowly dried out until it becomes a powdery consistency. The delicious taste makes it readily available for use in both savory and sweet dishes and can usually be found in any convenient store. Its subtle flavor makes it a great base for most dishes and acts as a binder for the other ingredients. Although it has the ability to absorb water and other liquid substances, it doesn't create moistness but rather allows other ingredients to form a dense consistency.

100 grams of coconut flour would include approximately 500 calories with 30 grams of carbs, 20 grams of protein, 5 grams of fat and 30 grams of fiber.

- **Flaxseed Flour**

Also known as linseed, flaxseed is a glossy brown seed[3] that is found in the plant of the same name. It contains a large number of health benefits and can even prevent and treat (according to research) some diseases and illnesses such as cancer and diabetes. The flour is made by simply grinding up the flaxseed until a powdery consistency is reached and can be used in most dishes on a daily basis. It has a nutty and earthy taste that is not too overpowering and can be used as a great alternative for wheat flour.

In 100 grams of flaxseed, you will find about 200 calories, 12 grams of fiber, 3 grams of carbs and 10 grams of protein.

Butter

The next essential ingredient in a keto kitchen is **butter[4]**. Due to its high fat amount, its caloric level is quite high (about 600 calories per 100 grams), and thus it should be used in moderation. Despite this, it still remains a source of good fat and can still be seen as a healthy and nutritional food. Since butter is essentially only made up of milk fat, it has virtually no carbs at all. This means it is a great flavorful addition to most keto-based recipes. Some of the kinds of butter that are more keto-friendly are:

- **Grass-fed Butter**

In contrast to grain-fed butter, grass-fed butter means that the cow has only eaten pure and fresh grass. This means that the milk it produced did not contain any other substances like chemicals or hormones that are usually found in grains. Due to the all-natural nature of grass-fed butter production, it becomes a healthier option to use. What makes it better is that it contains a higher amount of omega-3 fatty acids as well as a much higher amount of CLA (conjugated linoleic acid, which is an essential fatty acid

---

[3] (Magee, n.d.)
[4] (Hamzic, n.d.)

that allows the breakdown of fat and the building of muscle in the body) than usual grain-fed butter.

- **Ghee or Clarified Butter**

Clarified butter is the purest form of butter because it contains no milk or protein content. Once it has boiled down to pure butter, it becomes clarified and can be used for making dishes that can feed those who are lactose intolerant and vegan. Once the clarified butter burns down further to create a nuttier flavor and a longer shelf life (up to a year!), it becomes ghee. Ghee originates in India and is an excellent addition to baked goods.

A tablespoon (14 grams) of grass-fed butter or clarified butter will typically contain about 100 calories, 0.3 grams of cholesterol and no sugars or carbs.

Some butter brands to look out for:

1. Imported butter from Iceland called *Smjor* or from Germany called *Allgau*. Although their prices may seem a little steeper than other brands, if quality is what you're looking for, this is the brand to get. Both *Smjor* and *Allgau* are quality grass-fed butters which offer the most nutritional value.

2. If you're looking for another only grass-fed brand, *Organic Valley* is one of them. The downside here is that this butter is only produced in warmer weather so that the cows can be grass-fed. This means you may have to stock up on it for the colder seasons.

3. If, however, you're looking for the cheapest option, *Kerrygold* is the way to go. Even though the butter becomes grain-fed for the winter months, this butter is readily available all year round at a cheap price.

Sweeteners

Baking and snacking wouldn't be the same if there was no sweetness to some of the items. Sure, savory items are also deliciously fulfilling but there's just something about a crunchy little cookie that hits the sweet spot (pun intended). The next essential ingredient is **sweeteners**[5]. Some that are acceptable to use in the keto diet are:

- **Stevia**

Stevia is a substance obtained from a plant called *Stevia Rebaudiana.* What's great about it for the keto diet is the fact that it contains almost no carbs or fiber. You can purchase it from most convenient stores in both powdered and liquid form. When using it as a replacement for sugar, take care to substitute only 5 grams of Stevia for every 200 grams of sugar, this is because it is a lot sweeter than sugar and will unbalance your dish if you do not substitute it accordingly.

Stevia contains no nutritional value.

- **Erythritol**

This sugar-alcohol is used mainly because of its composition which prevents it from being fully absorbed as a sugar. This means that it carries fewer calories and also lowers the amount of sugar your body absorbs, so basically, you're getting a substance that tastes exactly like sugar, only it is much healthier! It can be readily substituted in all sugar recipes and can be purchased as a granulated substance, much like sugar at most health and baking stores.

In 100 grams of erythritol you will find about 350 calories as well as 80 grams of carbs.

- **Monk Fruit Extract**

As the name suggests, monk fruit extract is a substance extracted from a vine fruit called monk fruit. This fruit is made up of natural sugar compounds which are called mogrosides. The substance extracted from it contains no carbs or calories and this is

---

[5] (Link, 2018)

essential for maintaining a keto diet. It is a natural sweetener which can actually be up to 200 times sweeter than sugar! This means that substitutions should be made carefully with about half the amount of extract used in place of sugar. For instance, if a recipe requires 200 grams of sugar, you'd use 100 grams of monk fruit extract. This is, however, entirely up to you and the recipe you're following.

This extract contains no carbs, sugars or nutritional value.

- **Chicory Root Fiber**

Chicory is a beautiful lilac herbaceous plant which is commonly used as a tea grain, however, its roots are gaining attention due to their sweetening properties. The fiber extracted from chicory root is composed of almost 98% of soluble fiber. This means that it is an excellent addition to keto recipes not only because of its sweetening agent but also because it is quite healthy too. When using this, make sure to be more lenient than usual with liquid substances as chicory root extract tends to become gummy when exposed to moisture. It can be found in health stores and is usually packaged as a dark brown powder.

Chicory Root Fiber contains small amounts of fats but little to no carbs.

Yeast

For the keto diet, **nutritional yeast** is a great addition to recipes for bread and other baked goods. Unlike active yeast, nutritional yeast is inactive and contains many beneficial aspects. These include:

- High amounts of protein. If used in a daily keto snack, it can increase the amount of protein you take in on a daily basis.

- Vitamin B12, usually found in meat, is a vital vitamin that many cannot receive naturally due to their diet. Nutritional yeast, however, contains an enormous amount of it! In just one tablespoon, nutritional yeast contains 5 micrograms of B12 which is double the amount that the average adult needs on a daily basis.

- It is low in carbs and sugar making it by the ideal keto baking ingredient

- It helps with your digestion and it's also anti-viral

- It is gluten-free

Psyllium Husk Powder

Since this diet requires strictly gluten-free recipes and ingredients, and since we've been able to substitute most normal carb ingredients with keto-friendly ones, we should also be able to substitute gluten. This is where psyllium husk powder comes in. It is made from the seeds of plantago plants and is very fibrous. What's great about it is that it perfectly supplements gluten by acting exactly the way it does in recipes. Gluten acts as a glue to hold and combine ingredients and so does psyllium husk powder.

Keto Baking Powder

Baking powder typically contains a starch which helps the other ingredients in it (baking soda and cream of tartar) react to form air bubbles. These air bubbles are what make baked goods light and fluffy. On the keto diet, however, starches will drastically stop your ketosis and must be avoided at all costs. This is why when you're using keto baking powder, you make your own, leaving out the starch. This means that your homemade baking powder will contain one part baking soda to two parts cream of tartar, with the cream of tartar making up for the starch removed. This, however, will create a more acidic mixture but considering the fact that most recipes will call for only about a tablespoon of baking powder, the amount of acid it will produce isn't harmful or damaging to the recipe.

Eggs

Eggs are the glue that holds most baked dishes together, quite literally! They help to combine the dry and wet ingredients so that they become a consistent batter and they also help make the final product smooth and creamy. What's great about eggs for the keto diet is that they contain the tiniest amount of carbs which make up 0% of our daily value. A large egg of about 50g is about 70 calories, contains 180 micrograms of cholesterol, and varying amounts of good fats that make up about 5g in total. Not only is it a great baking ingredient it's also a really great item for the keto diet in general.

Milk

Cow's milk contains large amounts of lactose. Lactose is essentially carbs and sugar and therefore makes milk not so great for the keto diet. This is the case for all dairy milk, unfortunately, so don't think using skimmed milk or low-fat milk is okay for the keto diet. A cup of cow's milk contains about 10 grams of carbs and recipes usually call for more than just a cup, so imagine all the carbs you'd be adding in! There is a solution, however, and like flour, milk can be effectively and rather deliciously substituted[6] with:

- **Coconut Milk**

Although coconut milk may contain a few carbs (by a few I mean only one or two) it is still a good option and won't take you out of ketosis as long as it is unsweetened. Sweetened variants contain numerous additives that will undoubtedly increase your carb intake so it is best to stay away from them.

1 cup of coconut milk contains 45 calories, 1 gram of carbs, 1 gram of sugar and 4 grams of fat.

- **Hemp Milk**

Made from the hemp plant's seeds, hemp milk is a great substitute for the keto diet because of its zero carbohydrate content.

1 cup of hemp milk contains 60 calories and 45 grams of fat.

- **Soy Milk (Unsweetened)**

---

[6] (Siclait, 2019)

Made from soybeans, soy milk is a composition of oil, water, and protein. It is a by-product of tofu manufacturing and thus is readily available at most convenience stores. It is not as sweet as any of the other nut milks, however it is much creamier.

1 cup of soy milk contains 30 grams of calories, 2 grams of fat and 2 grams of carbs.

- **Almond Milk (Unsweetened)**

Most similar to the taste of regular cow's milk, almond milk is the most widely used apart from regular milk. It is made from a mixture of almonds and water and is a sweet and creamy consistency. It also has a number of health benefits because of its low amount of calories and high nutritional value. It is low on carbs and sugar and it is high in vitamin E, D, as well as calcium. It's also naturally lactose free and thus is a perfect replacement for regular milk.

1 cup of almond milk contains 30 calories, 3 grams of fat, 1 gram of sugar and 1 gram of carbs

- **Cashew Milk (Unsweetened)**

Made the same way as almond milk, cashew milk is packed full of nutrients and unsaturated fatty acids that are beneficial to heart, skin, and eye health. It has a subtle sweet and nutty flavor that is a great addition to most dishes.

1 cup of cashew milk is 35 calories, has 3 grams of fat, 1 gram of carbs and no sugar.

Flavor and Spice and Everything Nice

What will the world of food be without spices and flavors? Pretty bland, and pretty boring I think. Flavors play such a huge role in the taste of things that without them we wouldn't really taste much. From salt to pepper to cinnamon to chilies, the way we incorporate these extras into our dishes determine whether they will taste good or not. Luckily, many flavors and spices do not have much nutritional value or calories, and so this means that we can use them as much as we desire without feeling guilty and without hindering dietary progression.

When on a diet, especially one with restrictions, it's sometimes hard to follow strict rules and regulations when the food you have to eat is of a completely different kind that you're used to. One thing you can do to make food more familiar is to use spices and flavors that you are used to. The amount of flavors and spices and everything in between can sometimes be overwhelming though, and so it's important to have some of the basics for sweet and savory dishes. Below is a checklist of some of the basics everyone should have in their kitchen:

Sweet:

- Vanilla extract or essence

- Nutmeg (whole or powdered)

- Cinnamon powder

- Sesame seeds

- Chocolate (chips or slabs)

- Fruit essences (orange, pear, pineapple, mango etc.)

- Poppy seed

Savory:

- Salt

- Pepper

- Paprika

- Chili powder

- Thyme (fresh or powdered)

- Rosemary (fresh or powdered)

- Basil (fresh or powdered)

- Coriander (fresh or powdered)

- Mint

- Cumin seeds

- Cardamom

- Fennel seeds

- Ginger (fresh or powdered)

- Garlic (fresh or powdered)

- Turmeric

- Zests of citrus fruits

Fruits and Vegetables

Let's all take a moment to thank our parents were when they forced us to finish our vegetables or try to eat an apple a day. Most of the time it takes us far too long to realize how important fruits and vegetables are. This _ has been drilled into us from a really young age and it honestly comes as no surprise when looking at how beneficial they are to our bodies. They are rich in fiber and contain vitamins and nutrients that are essential for the smooth functioning of our internal systems. The types of fruits and vegetables that are best for us and are packed with antioxidants and fiber are usually the most pigmented ones. So, bright and bold colors should always be included in all meals whether it's breakfast, a snack, or supper.

When it comes to fruits, it becomes a little tricky because many fruits are sweet and this usually means they might have some sugar content. In order to avoid getting that sugar content from fruits and breaking your ketosis, it is advised that you opt for fruits that have a fairly low sugar content, and yes, they do exist. A fruit becomes a low carb fruit when its water and fiber content overpower its sugar content, making it less likely to be absorbed as a carbohydrate. Fruits are an essential part of a healthy diet because they are so packed with fiber and nutrients and they can also be very easily adapted into most meals and snacks. Some of them alone, serve as a whole meal themselves. Some low sugar content fruits are:

- Watermelon (low in carbs and packed with water content and vitamin A)

- Olives (high in oleic acid and monounsaturated fats)

- Lemon and lime (rich in vitamin C and maintains the pH level of the body)

- Coconut (high in nutrients and fiber)

- Strawberries, raspberries, blueberries, blackberries (packed with antioxidants and vitamin C and also have a low carb content)

- Avocados (low in carbs and high in monounsaturated fats)

- Cantaloupe (low in carbs and fructose)

- Peaches (low in carbs and high in antioxidants)

- Nuts like pecans, peanuts, pistachios, macadamia nuts, walnuts, hazelnuts, almonds (low in carbs and high in fiber but should be eaten in moderation)

Vegetables, specifically those with high fiber content, are an essential part of the keto diet. Incorporating them into your daily meals is what will ensure you get all the nutrients you need for the day. They are low in carbs and high in fiber, making them the ideal ingredient to turn to with most of your plant-based recipes.

Some important low-carb vegetables include[7]:

- Bell peppers (contain vitamins A and C and help reduce inflammation)

- Mushrooms (low in carbs and have anti-inflammatory properties)

- Spinach (keeps your heart and eyes healthy) and kale (extremely high in antioxidants)

- Celery (low in carbs and contains anti-cancer properties)

- Cauliflower (low in carbs and contains high amounts of vitamins C and K) and broccoli (contain vitamins C and K and can help reduce insulin resistance)

- Cucumbers (low in carbs and keeps your brain healthy)

- Green beans (contains a high amount of antioxidants)

- Brussel sprouts (may reduce the risk of cancer)

- Tomatoes (rich in potassium)

- Radishes (low in carbs and contain anti-cancer properties)

- Lettuce (contains vitamins A, C, and K and is also the vegetable with the lowest carbs!)

- Cabbage (high in vitamins C and K)

- Onions (lowers blood pressure and cholesterol levels)

- Zucchini (packed with nutritional value and low in carbs)

- Eggplant (contains antioxidants that protect the heart and brain)

---

[7] (Spritzler, 2018)

Baking Skills, Techniques, and Tools You Will Need

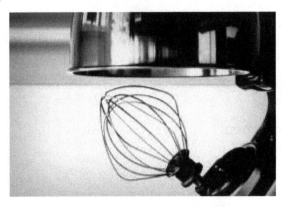

Baking is a highly addictive practice because of its therapeutic components. It all starts with deciding what to make, then preparing the ingredients, then actually making and seeing the finished production in all its glory is quite a fulfilling feeling. When you're so focused on making food, you tend to forget about other things and time passes quickly, which is why many people use cooking and baking as an escape from their busy, stressful lives. What this also means is that almost anyone can make a dish if they really want to. It's a simple application of knowledge and once you begin with the basics, you'll be sailing through most recipes in no time. Some things you need to become familiar with are baking skills and techniques that you may need as well as some of the tools that you will have to use. Knowing their names and purposes will allow you to put your knowledge to practice and hopefully create a beautifully delicious end product.

Here is a checklist of tools[8] and equipment you will need:

- ☐ An oven - hopefully you have an oven with which you're fairly familiar with. If not, it may take a few tries to get the temperatures and times correct but practice makes perfect. Although some dishes can be cooked in a microwave oven, the best results often come from using a simple conventional oven.

---

[8] (Beck, 2019)

☐ Measuring containers - whether cups, spoons, or jugs, these are essential to have when cooking or baking because most recipes call for precise measurements, so make sure you have enough containers to measure out more than one thing at a time.

☐ Spoons and spatulas - the three types of spoons or spatulas you will need are: a wooden spoon for stirring and mixing, a rubber spatula for mixing and scraping and a metal spatula for turning and removing finished products. You should buy more than one of each type so that you have enough to work with in case one is being used for something else already.

☐ Whisk - for whisking and mixing together both wet and dry ingredients

☐ Cooking brush - this is used to evenly coat dishes with grease before cooking and to lightly brush pastries and doughs with egg or butter before and after they hit the heat.

☐ Scissors - handy for opening ingredient packaging, cutting baking sheets, or quickly snipping ingredients.

☐ Rolling pin - to roll out doughs and crusts

☐ Sieve - to sift out dry ingredients as well as drain liquids from solids

☐ Knives - a whole variety of knives serve a whole variety of purposes. A big sharp chef's knife is used to slice and dice ingredients whereas smaller knives can be used to peel and de-skin ingredients

☐ Baking pans, tins, trays (for muffins and cupcakes), sheets (for cookies) and pots - usually come in different shapes and sizes which usually determine how long you have to bake certain things for, so make sure you have a nice variety to work with.

☐ Mixer - this can either be one that you hold yourself or one that stands on its own but either way it is very important to invest in one. It will come in handy to thoroughly mix and combine ingredients for batters and doughs.

☐ Parchment paper and baking spray - an essential part of preparation to ensure your goodies aren't ruined by sticking to their trays or tins.

☐ Aluminum foil - used to cover various dishes

☐ Grater and juicer - comes in handy when ingredients need to be grated or juiced

☐ Ramekins - handy for individually made dishes and are great for pies and puddings

☐ Digital scale - a huge time and effort saver that will give you precise measurements to ensure you have all your ratios correct

☐ Thermometer - to check internal temperatures of baked goods

Once you've been equipped with the above tools, it's important that you become familiar with a few of the very basic baking skills[9] and techniques[10]. The rest develop over time and become a natural part of how you go about your own individual way of doing things.

To get you started, here are a few preparatory skills you should start with:

- **Preheat the oven.** Almost all recipes call for a preheated oven and it should be the first thing that you look for in a recipe. It will usually give you a specific temperature to set the oven to, however if you are familiar with your oven and how it works, you can set it to whichever temperature you think will be sufficient.

---

[9] (King Arthur Flour Company, n.d.)
[10] ("basic baking techniques", n.d.)

Take care not to forget the preheating process because a lot of mixtures and batters tend to spoil if they are left waiting for the oven to heat up.

- **Prepare the baking tin.** Always use parchment paper or grease on tins before you add in your mixtures or batter. This will ensure that they do not stick to the tins and can be easily removed once baked or cooked.

- **Ensure your measurements are correct.** If you wish to get the perfect outcome of a sponge cake you have been dying to make, always make sure you follow the recipes measurements to a T. Some ingredients can be reduced in quantity or increased, however, it's always best to follow the quantities as they are given to ensure that your dish is perfectly balanced. For best results, do research if you are unsure about measurement conversions or use a scale to weigh out ingredients.

If you're going to be adding in fruits or vegetables into your cooking, it's likely that you'll read terms like *dice* or *slice* a few times. Here are the different culinary cuts you should look out for:

- **Dice** - to cut ingredients into tiny and uniform small cubes.

- **Cube** - to cut ingredients into larger uniform cubes.

- **Chop** - to roughly cut ingredients into bite size pieces.

- **Slice** - to thinly slice or cut across the grain of an ingredient, usually done with a serrated knife.

- **Julienne** - to cut the ingredients into long, thin strips.

- **Mince** - to cut ingredients into a very fine, almost paste-like consistency.

- **Chiffonade** - to cut leafy greens into thin, long ribbon-like pieces. Usually done by rolling up the leaves and then slicing them thinly.

Now, onto combining ingredients:

- **Creaming.** This process is the combination of whatever fat and whatever sugar source you're using. Usually it is butter and sugar and the mixture is creamed or mixed continuously until a light fluffy consistency is reached, often, the color will change as well from a yellow to a cream.

- **Whisking.** This process is when you whisk a liquid ingredient very rapidly to form a lighter more fluffier texture. Usually, egg whites are whisked until they become stiff peaks. You also whisk whole eggs before you scramble them. It can be done by hand with a whisk or by a mixer to save time and effort.

- **Folding.** This process serves to combine dry and wet ingredients all while keeping as many air bubbles in the mixture. It should be done with a whisk or flat spoon. In essence, you fold the dry ingredients into the wet by making large continuous circular movements from the bottom of the bowl up over the top of the ingredients.

- **Rubbing In.** This is when cold and solid butter is rubbed into flour so that you are able to coat very piece. The point isn't to mix and combine them into a cream or paste but rather to lightly rub them together until a course bread crumb consistency is achieved.

- **Kneading.** This is when you massage ingredients with your hands to make it combine as a smooth and well incorporated dough.

- **Mixing/Combining.** This, as the name suggests is the general practice of combining ingredients together. If the direction says mix well, it means all ingredients should be well mixed into each other. Sometimes it'll say roughly combine, and this would mean you would only mix for a few minutes and not too long or thoroughly.

- **Toss.** Here, you would usually shake around two ingredients so as to coat one with the other. Much like the way you toss a salad with its dressing or some popcorn with salt.

Once the ingredients are mixed and combined, it's time to bake the mixtures and combinations. Here's the techniques you need to know:

- **Baking.** Seems pretty basic, right? Sure, all you have to do is place whatever you're planning to bake into the preheated oven. Sometimes a recipe will require you to place the dish on the top tray or bottom tray, but if the recipe doesn't mention anything, it usually means it should be placed on the middle tray to ensure its uniformly baked. One thing to be cautious of is not opening your oven door too often, when you do, you allow the essential heat to escape and may find your dish picking up undesired qualities like rawness, being burnt or skimming in the middle.

- **Checking for doneness.** Ovens often vary, be it with their strengths or their ability to evenly cook, and due to this, the amount of time it'll take for a dish to be done will also vary, by maybe a few minutes. This is why it is important to check for doneness yourself. Usually a recipe will describe how the finished product should look and feel, but generally the color (from raw to brown to darker) and texture (from soft to firm to crispy) changes once the dish goes from being a mixture to a fully baked or cooked final product. For larger dishes, such as cakes or puddings, stick a skewer or thin knife in the middle and if it comes out clean with no wet bits still attached, your dish is ready.

- **Cooling.** When dishes come out of hot ovens, they still cook for a short period of time before they begin to fully cool down. To avoid this, it is important to transfer the baked goods onto a cooling rack so that it can cool down or stop cooking.

Once it is ready, to add an extra touch:

- **Melting chocolate.** This can be done using one of three methods, all of which require you to chop up the chocolate bar into small pieces. Once ready, you can either melt it:

  1. In the microwave, in a glass bowl for about 30 seconds until it is smooth and glossy.

  2. On the stove, in a saucepan, stirring continuously until it is fully melted and glossy.

  3. In a bowl over boiling water. The heat from the water is what will slowly melt the chocolate.

*Make sure you do not overheat or allow any water to get into the chocolate because it will cause it to split and spoil

Chapter 3: Time and Money Saving Tips

Starting and maintaining a diet is not only stressful for your mind and body, but your wallet too. Stocking up on new and specialized items specifically for your diet can cause a major consequences to your budget and so it's important to always find the cheapest way to go about it. Since this book focuses on baking bread and making snacks, the following list of time and money saving tips will be centered around how to save money and time when baking and preparing foods whilst on the keto diet. Here are some ways to do that:

- **Do it yourself.** Often, we opt for buying readymade packages of things just to save time, but we spend so much more money on things that are prepackaged than we think. In the case of salads, it's much more economical to buy your own fresh ingredients from a farmer's market rather than buy shelved products that could wilt and spoil at any time. Although it may take you a little more time to make the salad, you're going to get far better quality by doing it yourself.

- **Avoid wastage.** One way to ensure you get the most out of your time and money is to properly manage how you take care of your food. Once cooked, always store in airtight containers to ensure that the stored food lasts long and remains fresh. Another thing to consider is not preparing too much food at a time. Always make just enough so that you don't have store away too much food and risk it becoming stored away and forgotten.

- **Buy bulk.** For items that have a shelf life longer than three to four months, buy them in bulk. Things like spices, flour, and dried fruits and nuts can last a long time if properly stored and are much cheaper when bought in bulk rather than small quantities.

- **Grow your own.** Invest in a small herb garden in which you can grow your own fresh herbs and spices. It's not very difficult to maintain and can even be broadened to grow some vegetables like tomatoes and lettuce.

- **Plan ahead.** Create a meal plan for the week, that way you know exactly what to buy and when. Once you have it all written down, it gives you the opportunity to budget your money and also stock up on products you will need for the whole week instead of doing it every day.

Part 2: Keto Bread and Keto Snacks Recipes

Keto Bread

Chapter 4: Buns and Bagels

Keto Burger Buns

Time: 40 minutes

Yield: 12 buns

Ingredients:

- 1 cup coconut flour

- ¼ cup psyllium husk powder

- 1 ½ teaspoons Keto baking powder

- 1 teaspoon salt (table salt or sea salt)

- 2 large eggs

- 2 cups egg whites

- ¾ cup ghee

- ¾ cup warm water

Directions:

1. Preheat your oven to 350°F

2. In a food processor, add the eggs, egg whites, ghee and warm water and set aside on low speed to combine

3. While the wet ingredients combine, in a large bowl, add the coconut flour, psyllium husk powder, keto baking powder, and salt and mix well

4. Once the wet mixture is light and fluffy, slowly add it into the dry ingredients and mix well until a dough is formed. Divide the dough into 12 equal parts and with wet hands, form 12 round buns

5. Lightly grease a baking sheet and place the buns on, slightly pressing down on each one so they become flatter

6. Place into the oven and let them bake for 25 minutes or until slightly brown and cooked in the middle. Once done, allow them to cool on a baking tray, cut in half and fill with a juicy meaty beef patty and some lettuce and homemade mayo, or alternatively, fill with grated cheddar cheese and baby spinach leaves as a delicious keto lunch!

Savory Buns

Time: 40 minutes

Yield: 6 buns

Ingredients:

- ¾ cup almond flour

- 2 tablespoons psyllium husk powder

- 1 teaspoon keto baking powder

- ½ teaspoon garlic powder

- 1 tablespoon black and white sesame seeds

- ½ teaspoon salt (table salt or sea salt)

- 1 large egg

- 2 egg whites

- 1 tablespoon lemon juice

- 3 tablespoons melted ghee

- 4 tablespoons boiling water

Directions:

1. Preheat your oven to 350°F

2. In a bowl, mix the almond flour, psyllium husk powder, keto baking powder, garlic powder, sesame seeds, and salt together

3. In another bowl, whisk together the egg, egg whites, lemon juice, and ghee until light and fluffy

4. Pour the wet mixture into the dry one and combine thoroughly using a plastic spatula, whilst mixing, slowly pour in the boiling water which will further combine the ingredients

5. Once you form a dough, divide it into 6 pieces and shape them into balls with your hands

6. Line a baking tray with parchment paper and place the buns on

7. Bake for 30 minutes or until golden brown. Remove them from the tray and cool before serving. Can be served as a sandwich of leafy green salad tossed with balsamic vinegar, olive oil, and salt and vinegar as a delicious keto lunch

Bagels and Avo

Time: 30 minutes

Yield: 4 bagels

Ingredients:

- 2 cups almond flour

- 1 teaspoon nutritional yeast

- ¼ teaspoon salt

- ¾ cup warm water

- ⅓ cup unsweetened soy milk

- 1 teaspoon poppy seeds

- 1 avocado

- A handful of cherry tomatoes

- ¼ teaspoon black pepper

Directions:

1. Preheat your oven to 350°F

2. In a large bowl, mix almond flour, nutritional yeast, salt, and warm water until well incorporated and knead into an elastic dough

3. Bring some water to a boil in a large pot

4. While the water begins to boil, divide the bagel dough into 4 pieces and shape each one by making them into rounds, poking a hole in the middle and stretching out the dough until a bagel shape is formed

5. Once the water is boiling, reduce the heat until it begins to only just simmer and then place all 4 bagels into the water. Let it cook for 30 seconds on each side and then remove them

6. Line a baking tray with parchment paper and then place the bagels on top. Use the soy milk to lightly brush teach bagel and then sprinkle each one with poppy seeds.

7. Bake for 25 minutes or until golden brown and then put them onto a baking rack to cool

8. Brush each bagel with soy milk and sprinkle with seeds (you can use sesame seeds and poppy seeds)

9. While it cools, cut the avocado in half, remove the seed, and scrape all of it into a bowl. Mash it with a fork and add in the black pepper. Mix well and then thinly slice the cherry tomatoes

10. Once bagels have cooled, slice them in half (horizontally), smear some avocado on and then place a few slices of cherry tomatoes on top. Serve immediately!

Eggplant Bagels

Time: 40 minutes

Yield: 4 bagels

Ingredients:

- ⅓ cup coconut flour

- 1 teaspoon keto baking powder

- Salt (table salt or sea salt)

- 2 large eggplants

- 1 cup grated mozzarella cheese

- 2 large eggs

Directions:

1. Preheat your oven to 400°F

2. Peel the eggplants and then grate them finely. Sprinkle the eggplant with salt and then let it sit in a strainer for around 15 - 20 minutes to get rid of the liquid drainage

3. While it drains, combine the coconut flour, keto baking powder, ½ teaspoon salt as well as the eggs in a bowl until well incorporated

4. Place the mozzarella cheese in a small saucepan over medium heat and allow it to melt, and while it's still hot, add it to the bowl with the flour mixture and the grated eggplant and knead well until it forms a smooth dough

5. Spray a doughnut tray with cooking spray or brush it with melted butter. Divide the dough into 4 and then shape it around the tray. Alternatively, you can line a baking sheet with parchment paper and shape the dough into a bagel shape with your hands

6. Place the tray into the oven for 20 minutes or until the edges begin to brown, and serve immediately

Chapter 5: Bread Loaves

Almond Flour Bread with Parsley and Garlic Pesto

Time: 70 minutes

Yield: 18 slices (½ inch thick)

Ingredients for bread:

- 2 cups almond flour

- 1 tablespoon keto baking powder

- ¼ cup psyllium husk powder

- ½ teaspoon salt (table salt or sea salt)

- 1 tablespoon sesame seeds

- ¼ cup solid butter

- 4 large eggs

- ½ cup warm water

Ingredients for pesto:

- 2 ½ cups de-stemmed fresh parsley

- 3 cloves fresh garlic/2 tablespoons garlic powder

- ⅓ cup pine nuts

- ⅓ cup olive oil

- Salt and pepper to taste

Directions for bread:

1. Preheat your oven to 350°F

2. Combine the almond flour, keto baking powder, psyllium husk powder, and salt in a bowl and stir well

3. In a separate bowl, crack the eggs and beat them, melt the butter and add it in as well. Pour the water into the wet mixture and whisk well

4. Briefly fold in the wet mixture into the dry one, making sure there are a lot of air bubbles but at the same time, no clumps of dry ingredients

5. Generously line a loaf pan with parchment paper, making sure there is enough sticking out from the sides and then add in the bread batter

6. Grease your hands with some butter and shape the bread, rounding it at the top. Sprinkle the sesame seeds over and lightly press down on them to ensure they stick

7. Place the pan into the oven and bake for 60 minutes. To check if done, insert a thin knife into the center of the loaf, if it comes out clean, it's ready! The top layer might need a few extra minutes to become hardened like a bread crust

8. Allow the bread to cool fully before you slice into it

Directions for pesto:

1. Combine all the ingredients into a food processor and grind until smooth and even. Make sure to stop every 30 seconds to mix the bits that aren't being processed into the middle. Once completely smooth, transfer the pesto into an airtight jar and scoop some (about a teaspoon) onto a slice of bread. Spread it evenly and enjoy!

Coconut Flour Bread

Time: 80 minutes

Yield: 16 slices

Ingredients:

- 1 cup coconut flour

- ⅔ cup flaxseed flour

- 12 large eggs

- ¾ cup solid butter

- ¼ cup sesame seeds

- ¼ cup pumpkin seeds

- 2 tablespoons keto baking powder

- 1 teaspoon salt (table salt or sea salt)

Directions:

1. Preheat your oven to 325°F

2. Add the coconut flour, flaxseed flour, sesame and pumpkin seeds, keto baking powder and salt into a large bowl and whisk until well mixed

3. Melt the butter and then add it into the dry mixture. Combine well until all of the flour and butter have formed a crumbly texture

4. In a large bowl, crack all 12 of the eggs and whisk them together with an electric mixer until they have tripled in volume. You want the eggs to become as light and fluffy as possible

5. Once they are ready, fold the eggs into the dry mixture to form a batter. After a few minutes, the batter should thicken

6. Line a long loaf pan with parchment paper and allow some of the paper to hang off all sides to allow for easy removal once the bread is done

7. Pour the thickened batter into the pan, and sprinkle on a few more sesame and pumpkin seeds on top. Rub a tiny bit of butter on your hands and shape the bread with a slightly higher center to form a loaf-like shape.

8. Pop it into the oven and bake until it has browned on the top. It should rise significantly and take about 50 minutes to fully bake.

9. After 50 minutes, place some aluminum foil over the top and put it back into the oven for an additional 10 - 15 minutes so that the inside bakes until done. When done, use a thermometer to check the internal temperature of the bread, it should be around 170 F

10. The bread should cool in the pan, and the bread should be left alone until it fully cools down. Once cooled, you can use the parchment paper to easily lift the bread out of the pan. Slice the bread into ½ inch slices and eat or store in the refrigerator for up to 7 days

Keto Banana Loaf

Time: 70 minutes

Yield: 12 thick (¾ inch) slices

Ingredients:

- 2 cups almond flour

- ¼ cup coconut flour

- 1 tablespoon keto baking powder

- 1 tablespoon cinnamon powder

- ½ cup minced walnuts

- ¼ cup minced almonds

- ½ cup erythritol

- 6 tablespoons butter

- 1 tablespoon banana extract

- 4 large eggs

- ¼ unsweetened almond milk

Directions:

1. Preheat your oven to 350°F

2. In a large bowl, whisk together the almond flour, coconut flour, keto baking powder, cinnamon, and the minced walnuts and almonds

3. In a separate large bowl, using an electric mixer, cream the butter and erythritol on high speed. Once the mixture is light and fluffy, lower the speed, crack in the eggs, and combine well

4. Stir the almond milk and banana extract into the wet mixture and then add the dry mixture into the bowl as well. Thoroughly mix until a thick bread batter forms

5. Generously line a loaf pan with parchment paper (paper sticking out the edges) and then add in the batter. Smooth the batter down to make it even and then place it into the oven to bake for 60 minutes

6. To check for doneness, slide a thin knife into the middle and if it comes out clean, the loaf is ready

7. Ideally, let the loaf set for a whole day at room temperature before you can cut into it but if you wish to do it before, the loaf should cool completely in the pan and then you can slice it

Chapter 6: Pizza Crusts and Breadsticks

Coconut Flour Pizza Crust

Time: 30 minutes

Yield: 1 pizza crust

Ingredients:

- ⅓ cup coconut flour

- ¼ cup unsalted butter

- 3 large eggs

- 1 teaspoon keto baking powder

- ¼ teaspoon salt (table salt or sea salt)

Directions:

1. Preheat your oven to 350°F

2. In a bowl, combine the eggs and unsalted butter until smooth

3. In a separate bowl, combine the coconut flour, keto baking powder and the salt and whisk together until well mixed

4. Add in the dry ingredients into the wet and mix well until a soft dough is formed

5. On a pizza sheet, spray on some cooking spray or alternatively line it with a layer of parchment paper

6. Roll the dough onto the pizza sheet, making it about ½ inch thick. Ensure it is evenly rolled

7. Pop it into the oven to bake for 20 minutes or until it's slightly browned and crisp on top but still soft on the middle

8. If you wish to use it immediately, top it with your pizza toppings and then put it back into the oven for about 5 minutes. If you wish to store it, place it on a cooling rack to cool fully and then refrigerate for up to 7 days

Zucchini Pizza Crust

Time: 50 minutes

Yield: 1 pizza crust

Ingredients:

- ¼ cup almond flour

- 2 medium sized zucchini

- Salt (table salt or sea salt)

- 3 large eggs

- 1 cup grated mozzarella cheese

- 1 tablespoon dried rosemary

Directions:

1. Preheat your oven to 350°F

2. Grate the zucchini and then spread it out on a thin baking sheet, place it into the preheated oven for about 10 minutes so that it can slightly cook and become dry

3. In the meantime, combine the almond flour, eggs, mozzarella, rosemary, and ½ teaspoon of salt in a bowl and mix thoroughly, when the zucchini has dried out or after 10 minutes, incorporate it into the mixture as well and form a dough

4. Line a pizza sheet with parchment paper or alternatively grease a non-stick pizza pan and thinly roll out the dough onto it

5. Pop it into the oven for 20 minutes or until the dough is beginning to brown. Remove the zucchini pizza crust and add your toppings and then return it to the oven for about 10 more minutes. Slice up and enjoy!

Cheesy Breadsticks

Time: 30 minutes

Yield: 24 breadsticks

Ingredients for breadsticks

- ¾ cup almond flour

- 1 teaspoon keto baking powder

- 1 tablespoon psyllium husk powder

- 1 large egg

- ¼ cup cream cheese

- 2 cups grated mozzarella cheese

Ingredients for cheese topping:

- ¼ cup grated cheddar cheese

- ¼ cup shredded Parmesan cheese

- 1 teaspoon onion powder

- 1 teaspoon garlic powder

- ¼ teaspoon dried thyme

- A pinch of paprika

Directions:

1. Preheat your oven to 400°F and place the oven tray on the highest level

2. In a small mixing bowl, add the cream cheese and egg until slightly combined and then set it aside

3. In a larger bowl, tip in the almond flour, keto baking powder and the psyllium husk powder and stir until mixed

4. In a microwavable bowl, add the mozzarella cheese and microwave it until it starts to sizzle. Every 30 seconds, take it out and stir it so that all the cheese is incorporated into the melting process

5. Add in the cream cheese and egg mixture as well as the mozzarella cheese into the dry ingredients bowl. Mix well and knead it into a dough

6. Line a baking sheet with aluminum foil and press the dough flat until it covers the entire surface of the baking sheet. Use your hands and fingers to do this so that you're able to reach the tight edges and corners too. Set it aside for a few minutes

7. While the breadstick base is set aside, combine the cheddar cheese, parmesan cheese, onion and garlic powder, as well as the thyme and paprika in a bowl. Toss it so that all the cheese and spices are well mixed

8. Once the topping is done, sprinkle it all over the breadstick base and then thinly slice the base into the sizes you wish your breadsticks to be. With a thick top knife, slightly part each piece so that it can bake individually rather than as a whole baking sheet

9. Pop it into the oven for 15 minutes. The breadsticks should be crispy and the cheese topping should be slightly brown when it is ready. Serve warm and enjoy!

Cinnamon Sticks

Time: 35 minutes

Yield: 20 thin breadsticks

Ingredients:

- ½ cup almond flour

- ¼ cup coconut flour

- ¼ cup erythritol

- 1 teaspoon keto baking powder

- 2 tablespoons cinnamon powder

- 1 ½ cup grated mozzarella cheese

- ¼ cup + 3 tablespoons melted butter

- 1 large egg

- ½ teaspoon vanilla essence

- 1/2 tsp vanilla extract

Directions:

1. Preheat your oven to 350°F

2. In a large bowl, add the almond flour, coconut flour, erythritol and keto baking powder and mix well

3. On low heat, in a large skillet or saucepan, add the ¼ cup butter and mozzarella cheese until the cheese melts and they combine with each other. Once the cheese is melted but still has some visible streaks, add in the vanilla essence and the egg and stir well

4. Add the dry ingredients into the sauce pan and mix until a dough forms. Keep it on low heat for a minute or two

5. Take the dough off the heat and knead it on a flat surface for a few minutes until uniformly combined

6. Line a baking sheet with parchment paper

7. On the flat surface, roll out the dough into a large square about 50x50cm. Brush the rest of the butter all over the dough's surface and then evenly sprinkle the cinnamon over. Fold the dough in half, careful not to break or tear it. Roll out the folded dough a little flatter and cut into 20 even strips. The strips can be about 1 - 2cms thick

8. Place the strips onto the parchment lined baking sheet and bake for 15 minutes or until the sticks are golden brown and crispy. Serve with melted chocolate

Keto Snacks

Chapter 7: Muffins

Flaxseed Muffins

Time: 30 minutes

Yield: 12 muffins

Ingredients:

- 1 ¼ cup flaxseed flour

- 1 tablespoon coconut flour

- 1 tablespoon almond flour

- ½ teaspoon keto baking powder

- 1 teaspoon cinnamon powder

- ¼ teaspoon nutmeg powder

- ⅓ cup finely chopped pecans

- 1 teaspoon vanilla essence

- ⅓ cup melted butter

- 1 teaspoon lemon juice

- 4 large eggs

- 2 ½ teaspoons stevia

Directions:

1. Preheat your oven to 350°F

2. In a large mixing bowl, combine the flaxseed, coconut and almond flour, the baking powder, nutmeg and cinnamon powder, as well as the chopped pecans and mix them well

3. In another bowl, add the butter, stevia, vanilla essence, eggs, and lemon juice and whisk until light and smooth

4. Add the wet ingredients to the dry and stir until fully combined

5. Fill a muffin tray with cupcake liners and then drop in spoonfuls of muffin batter until the cups are ¾ full

6. Pop them into the oven for 15 minutes and then take them out and allow them to cool in the same pan for another 15 minutes

7. Serve with a layer of butter or cream and enjoy!

Berry Muffins

Time: 40 minutes

Yield: 12 muffins

Ingredients:

- 2 cups of almond flour

- ¼ cup coconut flour

- 1 tablespoon keto baking powder

- ¼ cup raspberries

- ¼ cup blueberries

- 6 mint leaves

- ½ cup erythritol

- 2 tablespoons melted butter

- ¼ cup unsweetened almond milk

- 1 teaspoon vanilla essence

- 5 large eggs

Directions:

1. Preheat your oven to 350°F

2. In a bowl, add the almond flour, coconut flour, erythritol, and keto baking powder and mix well

3. In a different bowl, use an electric mixer to beat the eggs, butter, vanilla essence, and almond milk on high speed

4. Once the wet ingredients are mixed thoroughly, add in the dry mixture and combine just enough to coat all the dry mix with the wet mix

5. Dice the raspberries and blueberries and chiffonade the mint leaves, toss them all into the muffin mixture and fold until well incorporated

6. Place cupcake liners into a muffin tray and fill them about ¾ way up with the muffin batter

7. Bake for 20 - 25 minutes or until they brown on the top. Once baked, remove from the tin and place on a baking tray to cool. Serve with butter or cream

Choc-Zucc Muffins

Time: 35 minutes

Yield: 12 muffins

Ingredients:

- 1 cup almond flour

- ½ cup cocoa powder

- ⅓ cup erythritol

- 1 teaspoon keto baking powder

- ¼ cup finely grated pecan nuts

- 1 small sized zucchini

- ½ cup butter

- 3 large eggs

- 1 tablespoon vanilla essence

- Salt to taste

Directions:

1. Preheat your oven to 350°F

2. Grate the zucchini, lightly sprinkle it with salt and leave to drain for 10 minutes

3. While the zucchini drains, combine the almond flour, cocoa powder, erythritol, and keto baking powder in a large bowl and mix together well

4. In a separate bowl, whisk together the eggs, butter, and vanilla essence. Place the zucchini on a fine mesh cloth or a clean dish cloth, squeeze until all liquid is out and then add it to the wet mixture.

5. Pour the wet ingredients into the dry and combine well

6. Line a muffin tray with cupcake holders and fill them ¾ way up with the delicious chocolate zucchini muffin batter. Top each one with finely grated pecan nuts

7. Place it into the oven and bake for 20 minutes, use a toothpick to check for doneness and then cool on a baking rack

Chapter 8: Cookies

Coconut Cookies

Time: 40 minutes

Yield: 16 cookies

Ingredients:

- 1 cup almond flour

- ½ cup shredded coconut

- ¼ erythritol

- A pinch of salt

- 3 large egg whites

- 3 tablespoons melted butter

- 1 teaspoon liquid stevia

Directions:

1. Preheat your oven to 350°F

2. In a large bowl, mix together the almond flour, coconut, erythritol, and salt until well combined

3. In a smaller bowl, whisk together the egg whites, butter, and stevia and then add into the dry ingredients

4. Stir in the wet ingredients until a soft and smooth cookie dough is achieved

5. Line a baking a baking sheet with parchment paper and lightly grease the top of the paper with butter

6. Roll into a ball about a tablespoon of cookie dough in the palms of your hands and then place them on the tray. Use a fork to lightly press down on them, causing them to flatten, giving them a fork shaped decoration

7. Pop them in the oven for 20 minutes or until they begin to brown around the edges

8. Use a metal spatula to scoop up one cookie at a time and place them on a cooling rack

9. Serve on unsweetened vanilla ice cream or with a chocolate dip

Choc-chip Cookies

Time: 30 minutes

Yield: 12 big cookies

Ingredients:

- 1 ½ cup almond flour

- ½ teaspoon keto baking powder

- ½ cup erythritol

- 1 tablespoon powdered gelatin

- ½ cup dark chocolate chips

- ½ cup melted butter

- 1 tablespoon vanilla essence

- 2 large eggs

Directions:

1. Preheat your oven to 350°F

2. In a large bowl, mix together the almond flour, keto baking powder, erythritol, gelatin, and chocolate chips

3. In a smaller bowl, beat the eggs, butter, and vanilla essence until well combined

4. Stir in the wet ingredients into the dry mixture until fully incorporated into a slightly stiff cookie dough

5. Line a baking sheet with a layer of parchment paper

6. Roll the dough into 12 even balls, and place them onto the sheet. Press down on them until they spread out into rounds about the radius of a cup

7. Bake them for 20 minutes or until the edges become firm. Remove from the oven and let them cool on the baking sheet, the centers will continue cooking as they cool down

8. Serve with cooled almond milk

Caramel Cookies

Time: 30 minutes

Yield: 12

Ingredients for the cookies:

- 2 cups almond flour

- 1 cup softened coconut butter

- ⅓ cup erythritol

- A pinch of salt

- 1 teaspoon vanilla essence

Ingredients for the caramel:

- 2 tablespoons ghee

- ½ cup erythritol

- ⅓ coconut cream

Directions:

1. Preheat your oven to 350°F

2. Cream the butter and erythritol until light and smooth. Add in the salt and vanilla essence and mix until fully combined

3. Once fully combined, add in the almond flour to create a firm dough. Transfer it into a piece of cling film and roll it into a log. Place it in the fridge to set further

4. For the caramel, combine the ghee and erythritol in a small saucepan over medium heat. Wait until the erythritol melts and then add in the coconut cream. Let the mixture cook on medium until it begins to thicken and get sticky. Remove it from the heat and allow it to cool whilst occasionally stirring it

5. Line a baking sheet with parchment paper

6. Pull out the chilled dough from the freezer and slice the log into 12 even pieces. Further shape the cookies so that they're nice and round and then place them on the baking sheet

7. Pop them in the oven for about 15 minutes or until the edges start to brown. Once they're done, let them cool on the baking sheet

8. Take 6 cookies, and spread on a layer of caramel, then sandwich it with another cookie. Press down until the caramel drips out the sides of the cookies. Allow to set for a few minutes and then serve

Chapter 9: Additional Assorted Snacks

Cheese Scones

Time: 30 minutes

Yield: 15 scones

Ingredients:

- 1 ½ cup almond flour

- ¼ cup coconut flour

- ¼ cup flaxseed flour

- 1 teaspoon keto baking powder

- ¼ cup unsweetened almond milk

- 3 large eggs

- ½ cup grated cheddar cheese

- 3 tablespoons finely chopped chives

- ½ teaspoon ground black pepper

- ¼ teaspoon salt (table salt or sea salt)

- 1 teaspoon dried thyme

Directions:

1. Preheat your oven to 380°F

2. In a large bowl, combine the almond flour, coconut flour, flaxseed flour, keto baking powder, cheddar cheese, and the chives until evenly mixed

3. In a smaller bowl, whisk 2 eggs and the almond milk together

4. Combine the eggs and milk with the dry mixture until fully incorporated into a slightly sticky dough

5. It's sticky consistency will not allow you to roll it with just a rolling pin, so sandwich the dough between two pieces of parchment paper and roll it out until it's about ½ an inch thick. Remove the upper parchment paper and use a cookie cutter to cut out rounds. Place the rounds on a baking sheet lined with parchment paper. Keep rolling out the dough until you've shaped all the dough. Alternatively, you could shape the dough with your hands. Simply divide the dough into 15 pieces and round them up between your palms

6. Beat the remaining egg in a cup and lightly brush the eggs with it using a cooking brush. Lightly sprinkle the dried thyme over each scone and place it into the oven for 15 - 20 minutes. Once ready, the scones will brown and become crispy at the top.

7. Allow to cool for 10 minutes and serve with butter

Keto Pasta

Time: 60 minutes

Yield: Dependent on the type of pasta you shape it into

Ingredients:

- 1 cup almond flour

- 4 tablespoons coconut flour

- 2 teaspoons garlic powder

- ¼ teaspoon salt

- 1 large egg

- 2 teaspoons lemon juice

- Water as needed

- ¼ cup butter

- 2 tablespoons coconut oil

Directions:

1. In a food processor or dough maker, add in the almond flour, coconut flour, and salt until they mix. While it mixes, pour in the lemon juice and allow it to become evenly distributed

2. Lightly beat the egg and add it into the mixture as well. As the mixture combines add in teaspoons of water as needed until the mixture begins forming a dough. The correct texture of the dough should be firm but sticky. Alternatively, you can knead the dough until it reaches the right texture

3. You can then wrap the dough up in cling wrap/cling film and knead it whilst wrapped

4. This dough can be stored for up to a week inside the refrigerator or used right away. You can make a number of pastas using it such as farfalle, orecchiette, or cavatelli. It all depends on which type of shape you favor best. Once you shape it it's ready to be cooked

5. To cook the pasta, heat a skillet or frying pan over low heat. Melt the butter and oil and then add in the pasta and allow it to cook until it slightly changes color. Serve immediately with the topping or sauce of your choice

Keto Crackers

Time: 60 minutes

Yield: 30 crackers

Ingredients:

- ⅓ cup almond flour

- 2 tablespoons psyllium husk powder

- ⅓ cup sesame seeds

- ⅓ cup pumpkin seeds

- 1 teaspoon salt (table salt or sea salt)

- ¼ cup coconut oil

- 1 cup boiling water

Directions:

1. Preheat your oven to 300°F and place your oven tray on the lowest level

2. In a large bowl, add the almond flour, psyllium husk powder, salt, sesame and pumpkin seeds and combine well with a wooden spoon

3. Rub in the coconut oil and start to combine well. Use the boiling water to combine all ingredients into a dough that has a gel-like consistency

4. Line a baking tray with parchment paper and add on the dough. Use your hands to flatten or alternatively cover it with another piece of parchment paper and roll it out with a rolling pin and then remove the parchment paper

5. Once flattened, place the tray into the oven and bake for about 40 minutes or until crackers have browned and turned crispy. Allow to fully cool before you break the crackers into smaller pieces

Cupcakes

Time: 45 minutes

Yield: 12 cupcakes

Ingredients:

- 1 cup almond flour

- ¼ cup coconut flour

- ¼ teaspoon salt (table salt or sea salt)

- 1 teaspoon keto baking powder

- 4 tablespoons coconut butter

- ½ cup erythritol

- 1 tablespoon vanilla essence

- 4 large eggs

Directions:

1. Preheat your oven to 350°F

2. Cream the butter and erythritol in a bowl. Ensure the erythritol is fully dissolved and the mixture is light and creamy. Once this is achieved, add in the vanilla essence and the eggs and mix well with a whisk

3. Sift in the almond and coconut flour, keto baking powder, and salt into the wet mixture. Mix until just combined. Do not over mix

4. Place cupcake liners into a muffin tray and spoon in the cupcake batter until the cups are ¾ full. You may add a topping on top of the cupcake batter like finely chopped pecan nuts or raspberries or alternatively ice the cupcakes once they come out of the oven and have cooled

5. Bake for about 30 minutes or until the cupcakes are slightly browned and have passed the doneness test. Let them cool fully before you remove the liners and frost

Chapter 10: Keto Fat Bombs

Cream Cheese Fat Bombs

Time: 70 minutes

Yield: 15 fat bombs

Ingredients:

- 1 cup heavy cream

- 1 cup cream cheese

- 4 tablespoons erythritol

- 2 teaspoons vanilla essence

- ¼ cup finely chopped walnuts

- ¼ cup finely chopped raspberries

Directions:

1. In a bowl, add the cream cheese, erythritol, and vanilla essence and mix with an electric mixer until fully incorporated. Allow it to sit for a few minutes so that the erythritol can dissolve fully

2. Add in the heavy cream, half a cup at a time, mix on high, and pause between 15 second intervals to stir in the bits off the side. Add in the rest of the heavy cream and mix on low until the mixture begins to thicken and form peaks

3. Add in the walnuts and raspberries and stir well. Spoon the mixture into a piping bag

4. Line a baking sheet with parchment paper and pipe small rounds onto the sheet, the mixture should be enough for about 15 medium sized (about 3cm) fat bombs.

Place the sheet into the fridge to set for at least an hour before you can dig in. Keep refrigerated if there are any extras

Pineapple and Pecan Fat Bombs

Time: 70 minutes

Yield: 12 fat bombs

Ingredients:

- ½ cup coconut cream

- 2 tablespoons gelatin

- 3 tablespoons erythritol

- 2 teaspoons pineapple essence

- ½ cup boiling water

- ¼ cup finely chopped pecan nuts

Directions:

1. In a heatproof jug, add the gelatin and erythritol into the boiling water and stir until they've completely dissolved

2. Add the pineapple essence, coconut cream and pecans and combine thoroughly

3. Pour the mixture into a silicone mold that makes 12 and place it into the refrigerator for an hour before you can pop them into your mouth for a flavor explosion! Keep any extras refrigerated

Blueberry-Lemon Fat Bombs

Time: 70 minutes

Yield: 12 fat bombs

Ingredients:

- 1 cup cream cheese

- 4 tablespoons sour cream

- 3 tablespoons erythritol

- 2 tablespoons lemon juice

- The zest of 1 lemon

- 12 blueberries

Directions:

1. In a bowl, add the cream cheese, sour cream, erythritol, lemon juice, and lemon zest and use an electric mixer to combine fully. Let the mixture rest for a minute to allow the erythritol to dissolve and become fully incorporated

2. Use a small spoon to scoop up and fill up a silicone mold that makes 12. Fill each cup up halfway and then place a blueberry in the middle. Spoon more of the mixture into the cup until each mold is filled and each blueberry is covered

3. Place the mold into the refrigerator for an hour before you can serve them. Keep refrigerated

Chapter 11: Keto-Friendly Pre- and Post- Workout Snacks

In regard to working out, it is commonly suggested that you need to be fully nourished with a good amount of carbs in order to perform to the best of your ability. This is due to the misconception that you need the energy from carbs to give you the ability to work out. This would mean that people on the Keto diet wouldn't be able to work out or exercise, which is wrong. In fact, a study[11] showed that both normal carb eaters and low carb, keto diet followers performed at exactly the same level. The finding was due to the fact that once you begin the keto lifestyle, your body adapts to using fat as an energy source, and thus is able to function properly whilst a workout regime is introduced. Even though this is the case, if you're going to engage in any type of exercise, it's always important to keep yourself well-nourished and hydrated even if you're on the keto diet. Below are some delicious snack ideas for pre- and post- workout sessions:

Pre-Workout Session Snacks:

Keep them light on carbs, but still filled with some fat and fiber.

- Keto bars (pre-made, easy to obtain and eat on the go before a session at the gym)

- Fresh berries (eating a handful with some yoghurt will keep you sustained throughout your workout regime)

---

[11] ("Take Your Training to the Next Level with Ketosis", n.d.)

- A big bowl of leafy green salad (one can never go wrong with leafy greens, plus, it is packed with nutritional value that will keep you hydrated and refreshed throughout your workout!)

- Unsweetened, low-fat yoghurt or cream cheese (snack on them together with some keto crackers for an extra edge)

- Keto fat bombs (a great source of delicious fat to keep you going strong all session. See recipes above)

Post-Workout Session Snacks

Keep them high in protein and fat[12]

- Whey protein shake (because whey protein is a complete protein, it includes all 9 essential amino acids, meaning it is really good for you!)

- Grass-fed meat and fish (meals including these excellent sources of fat and protein will ensure you have all you need after a tough day at the gym)

- Eggs (scrambled, poached or benedict style, eggs are a brilliant source of high fat and low carbs)

- Coconut oil or butter (a great source of MCT - a type of fat that pushes you into ketosis. Include the oil in your protein shakes and the butter in your meals)

- Green vegetables (packed with nutrients your body starves for after a workout)

---

[12] (Stanton, 2018)

Conclusion

Hopefully, all of these amazing recipes are an inspiration for you to start and maintain your keto diet. Not only will they make you feel a little more familiar with regard to your meals and fill a gap for all the carbs you've cut down on but they'll also be a delicious and nutritious addition to your diet!

References

basic baking techniques. Retrieved from

https://stonesoupvirtualcookeryschool.com/2011/04/basic-baking-techniques/

Beck, A. (2019). https://www.bhg.com. Retrieved from

https://www.bhg.com/recipes/how-to/bake/essential-baking-tools/

Hamzic, H. Keto Nutrition - Calories in Butter & Other Nutrition Info. Retrieved from

https://www.kissmyketo.com/blogs/nutrition/keto-nutrition-calories-in-butter-other-info#

King Arthur Flour Company, I. Baking Tips & Techniques | King Arthur Flour.

Retrieved from https://www.kingarthurflour.com/learn/tips-and-techniques.html

Link, R. (2018). The 6 Best Sweeteners on a Low-Carb Keto Diet (And 6 to Avoid).

Retrieved from https://www.healthline.com/nutrition/keto-sweeteners

Magee, E. The Benefits of Flaxseed. Retrieved from

https://www.webmd.com/diet/features/benefits-of-flaxseed

Mawer, R. (2018). The Ketogenic Diet: A Detailed Beginner's Guide to Keto. Retrieved

from https://www.healthline.com/nutrition/ketogenic-diet-101#weight-loss

Siclait, A. (2019). Your Milk Consumption Might Be Sabotaging Your Keto Diet Weight Loss. Retrieved from https://www.womenshealthmag.com/weight-loss/a26326620/keto-milk/

Spritzler, F. (2016). 7 Effective Tips to Get Into Ketosis. Retrieved from https://www.healthline.com/nutrition/7-tips-to-get-into-ketosis

Spritzler, F. (2018). The 21 Best Low-Carb Vegetables. Retrieved from https://www.healthline.com/nutrition/21-best-low-carb-vegetables

Stanton, B. (2018). Top 10 Keto Post Workout Foods To Help You Build Muscle. Retrieved from https://perfectketo.com/keto-post-workout/#4

Take Your Training to the Next Level with Ketosis. Retrieved from https://blog.bulletproof.com/take-your-training-to-the-next-level-with-ketosis/

Keto Dessert & Chaffle Cookbook 2021 with Pictures

By

Keto Flex Academy

Table of Contents

Introduction

The ketogenic diet or Keto is a low-carbohydrate, mild protein, high-fat diet that will help you lose fat more efficiently. It has several advantages for weight reduction, wellbeing, and efficiency, so a rising number of healthcare professionals & practitioners recommend it.

Fat as a form of nutrition

For nutrition, the body uses three fuel sources: carbohydrates, fats and proteins. Carbohydrates convert into blood sugar or glucose in the bloodstream and are the primary fuel source for the body. If carbohydrates are not accessible, your body then depends on fat as an energy source. Protein is the primary building block of muscles and tissues. Protein could also be processed into glucose in a pinch and utilized for energy.

The keto diet encourages your body to utilize fat as the primary source of nutrition instead of carbohydrates, a ketosis mechanism. You consume too little carbs on the keto diet that the body cannot depend on glucose for nutrition. And your body turns to utilize fat for energy rather than carbs, as keto foods are filled with fat. A major part of the calories, almost 70 to 80% come from fat, consuming 15 to 20% of calories from protein and barely 5% calories from carbohydrates (that makes for about 20 to 30 grams of carbohydrates per day, depending on the weight and height of a person).

Meal options in regular diets

To conquer the weight reduction fight, it becomes tough to continue the dieting combat for a long period. Many people revert to the previous eating patterns after only a few weeks when confronted with the difficulty and limited food ranges of many diets, especially vegan, low-fat and low-calorie diets. For starters, the ketogenic diet is incredibly beneficial for weight reduction, but following specific food choices can be overwhelming. Only after three weeks can you begin noticing significant effects; however, the complications and inconvenience of transitioning to an effective ketogenic diet may deter you from keeping to the program long enough to reap the benefits.

Thankfully, to render your keto diet ever more efficient, successful and simple to use, you will build an array of foods, preparing strategies, tips and suggestions. One hidden tool can be used from the diet's outset, without much details of the keto diet, which is continued even after achieving the weight loss target.

That hidden preferred weapon is the "Fat Bomb."

The Fat Bomb

The fat bombs in the keto diet play a major role in motivation for the dieters. Indulging in a high fat dessert gives you a stress-free environment to continue your diet. These fat bombs provide the correct amounts of fat, carbohydrates, and protein resulting in weight reduction while supplying the user with sustained energy. They do this by supplementing your diet with chemicals that hold your body in a fat-burning state, even after you have had a fulfilling meal.

The Keto diet aims to rely on foods that are high in fat and low in carbs. By modifying what the body utilizes as food, it helps facilitate weight reduction. Carbohydrates, like those present in sugars and bread, are usually transformed into energy. If the body cannot have enough nutrients, the body begins to burn fat as a substitute for energy.

Your liver converts the fat into ketones, which are a form of acid. Getting a certain amount of ketones in your body will lead you to a biochemical condition known as ketosis. Your body can burn stored fat for fuel; thus, you will losing weight when you go through ketosis.

To reach a ketosis condition, it takes between one to ten days of consuming a low-carb, high-fat diet; to sustain the fat-burning cycle of ketosis, you have to continue consuming the keto diet. Eating fatty foods will help you more easily get into ketosis and sustain it for longer periods.

Fat bombs are 90% fat, making them the ideal keto addition for beginners and lifetime keto adherents. They hold you in a ketosis state and can provide health advantages unlike many other high protein foods; you can snack on fat bombs or have them as dinners or as have as a side dish too. They are simple to produce and are available in a range of varieties, from sweet to savory.

Can Fat Bombs Be Healthy?

Ketogenic fat bombs are fueled by two major ingredients: high-fat dairy and coconut oil. Both of these components have several powerful health advantages. Coconut produces a form of fat known as MCTs (medium-chain triglycerides), which gives the body additional ketones that can be readily consumed and used to sustain ketosis.

There are distinct health advantages of consuming high-fat dairy fat bombs. High-fat dairy products produce fatty acids known as CLA (conjugated linoleic acid), minerals and vitamins. Data indicates that CLA plays a significant role in the body's breakdown of fat and may lower cardiac attack and stroke risk.

Eating high-fat dairy meals prior to bedtime may help burn fat when still sleeping. Fat burned while you sleep the body with an energy that does not need to metabolize stress hormones or depend on sugar.

Keto Diet and Mood

There are various comments from individuals on a keto diet that probably indicate the association between the keto diet and mood changes. Various hypotheses connect the keto diet to mood regulation, even if only partly.

The explanation of why the keto diet aids in accelerated weight reduction and reversal of multiple chronic weight-related problems lead people to come out of the despair of "I am not healthy." As a consequence of the results themselves, most people report a positive attitude by adopting a keto diet. But is that important? What makes a difference is that it has a positive and long-lasting effect. Some research also shows that a ketogenic diet may help combat depression since it provides anti-inflammatory benefits. Inflammations are associated with, at least certain, forms of depression. A few of the advantages are provided below that create the relationship between the keto diet and mood. A keto diet:

1. Helps regulate energy highs and lows.

Ketones offer an immediate energy supply for your brain since they are metabolized quicker than glucose. Ketones give a long-lasting, more accurate and reliable energy supply, and when your body understands it can access your fat reserves for food as well, the brain does not worry.

2. Neurogenesis improvement

Dietary consumption is a crucial element in assessing neurogenesis. A reduced degree of neurogenesis is correlated with multiple depressive illnesses. On the other side, a higher rate increases emotional endurance.

3. Reduces and Brings Down Inflammation

The Keto Diet provides healthy nutritional options, so you avoid consuming inflammatory and refined products. Consuming anti-inflammatory food can have a direct impact on the attitude. If you eat nutritious food high in protein, healthy fats and low-carb vegetables, it reduces inflammation.

4. Feeds the brain.

The good fat you consume on Keto fuels your brain and stabilizes your mood. As your brain is composed of 60% fat, it requires an excess of healthy fats to function properly.

So go ahead and try these easy to make lo carb hi fat desserts and lose weight deliciously!

Chapter 1- Low Carb Desserts

1. 10 Minutes Chocolate Mousse

Prep. Time: 10 minutes

Servings: 4

The serving size is ½ cup

Nutrition as per serving:

218 kcal / 23g fat / 5g carbs / 2g fiber / 2g protein = 3g net carbs

Ingredients

- Powdered sweetener 1/4 cup

- Cocoa powder, unsweetened, sifted 1/4 cup

- Vanilla extract 1tsp.

- Heavy whipping cream 1 cup

- Kosher salt 1/4tsp.

Directions

With an electric beater, beat the cream to form stiff peaks. Put in the sweetener, cocoa powder, salt, vanilla and whisk till all ingredients are well combined.

2. The Best Keto Cheesecake

Prep. Time: 20 minutes

Cook Time: 50 minutes

Setting Time: 8 hours

Servings: 12

The serving size is 1 slice

Nutrition as per serving:

600kcal / 54g fat / 7g carbs / 2g fiber / 14g protein = 5 g net carbs

Ingredients

Layer of crust

- Powdered sweetener 1/4 cup

- Almond flour 1 1/2 cups

- Butter melted 6 tbsp.

- Cinnamon 1tsp.

Filling

- Cream cheese, full fat, room temperature (8 oz.)

- Powdered Sweetener 2 Cups

- Eggs at room temperature 5 Large

- Sour cream at room temperature 8 Oz.

- Vanilla extract 1 Tbsp.

Directions

1. Heat the oven to 325F.

2. Arrange the rack in the center of the oven. Mix dry ingredients for the crust in a medium mixing bowl. Mix in the butter. Transfer the crust mixture into a springform pan (10-inch x 4- inch), and using your fingers, press halfway up and around the sides. Then press the mixture with a flat bottom cup into the pan. Chill the crust for about 20 minutes.

3. Beat the cream cheese (at room temperature) in a large mixing container, with an electric beater or a

4. Hand mixer until fluffy and light.

5. If using a stand mixer, attach the paddle accessory.

6. Add in about 1/3rd of sweetener at a time and beat well.

7. Add in one egg at a time beating until well incorporated.

8. Lastly, add in the sour cream, vanilla and mix until just combined.

9. Pour this cheesecake mixture onto the crust and smooth out the top. Place in the heated oven and examine after 50 minutes. The center should not jiggle, and the top should not be glossy anymore.

10. Turn the oven off and open the door slightly, leaving the cheesecake inside for about 30 minutes.

11. Take out the cheesecake and run a knife between the pan and the cheesecake (this is to unstick the cake but don't remove the springform yet). Leave for 1 hour.

12. Chill for at least 8 hrs. loosely covered with plastic wrap.

13. Take off the sides of the springform pan, decorate & serve.

Note: all the ingredients to make the cheesecake should be at room temperature. Anything refrigerated must be left out for at least 4 hrs.

3. Butter Pralines

Prep. Time: 5 minutes

Cook Time: 11 minutes

Chilling Time: 1 hour

Servings: 10

The serving size is 2 Butter Pralines

Nutrition as per serving:

338kcal / 36g fat / 3g carbs / 2g fiber / 2g protein = 1g net carbs

Ingredients

- Salted butter 2 Sticks
- Heavy Cream 2/3 Cup
- Granular Sweetener 2/3 Cup
- Xanthan gum ½ tsp.
- Chopped pecans 2 Cups
- Sea salt

Directions

1. Line parchment paper on a cookie sheet with or apply a silicone baking mat on it.

2. In a saucepan, brown the butter on medium-high heat, stirring regularly, for just about 5 minutes.

3. Add in the sweetener, heavy cream and xanthan gum. Stir and take off the heat.

4. Add in the nuts and chill to firm up, occasionally stirring, for about 1 hour. The mixture will become very thick. Shape into ten cookie forms and place on the lined baking sheet, and sprinkle with the sea salt, if preferred. Let chill until hardened.

5. Keep in a sealed container, keep refrigerated until serving.

4. Homemade Healthy Twix Bars

Prep. Time: 5 minutes

Cook Time: 20 minutes

Servings: 18 Bars

The serving size is 1 Bar

Nutrition as per serving:

111kcal / 7g fat / 8g carbs / 5g fiber / 4g protein = 3g net carbs

Ingredients

For the cookie layer

- Coconut flour 3/4 cup
- Almond flour 1 cup
- Keto maple syrup 1/4 cup
- Sweetener, granulated 1/2 cup
- Flourless keto cookies 1/4 cup
- Almond milk 1/2 cup

For the gooey caramel

- Cashew butter (or any seed or nut butter) 1 cup
- Sticky sweetener of choice 1 cup
- Coconut oil 1 cup
- For the chocolate coating
- Chocolate chips 2 cups

Directions

1. Line parchment paper in a loaf pan or square pan and set aside.

2. In a big mixing bowl, put in almond flour, coconut flour, and then granulated. Combine very well. Mix in the keto syrup and stir to make it into a thick dough.

3. Add the crushed keto cookies and also add a tbsp. of milk to keep it a thick batter. If the batter stays too thick, keep adding milk by tablespoon. Once desired consistency is achieved, shift the batter to the prepared pan and smooth it out. Chill.

4. Combine the cashew butter, coconut oil and syrup on the stovetop or a microwave-safe dish and heat until mixed. Beat very well to make sure the coconut oil is completely mixed. Drizzle the caramel over the prepared cookie layer and shift to the freezer.

5. When the bars are hard, take out of the pan and slice into 18 bars. Once more, put it back in the freezer.

6. Liquefy the chocolate chips by heat. Using two forks, dip each Twix bar into the melted chocolate till evenly covered. Cover all the bars with chocolate. Chill until firm.

5. Best Chocolate Chip cookie

Prep. Time: 5 minutes

Cook Time: 20 minutes

Servings: 15 Cookies

The serving size is 1 Cookie

Nutrition as per serving:

98kcal / 6g fat / 12g carbs / 5g fiber / 5g protein = 7g net carbs

Ingredients

- Almond flour blanched 2 cups
- Baking powder 1 tsp
- Cornstarch 1/4 cup

- Coconut oil 2 tbsp.

- Sticky sweetener, keto-friendly 6 tbsp.

- Almond extract 1 tsp

- Coconut milk, unsweetened 1/4 cup

- Chocolate chips 1/2 cup

Directions

1. Heat oven up to 350F/175C. Line parchment paper on a large cookie tray and put it aside.

2. Place all the dry ingredients in a big mixing bowl, and combine well.

3. Melt the keto-friendly-sticky sweetener, almond extract and coconut oil in a microwave-safe proof or stovetop. Then mix it into the dry mixture, adding milk to combine very well. Stir through your chocolate chips.

4. Form small balls with slightly wet hands from the cookie dough. Set the balls up on the lined cookie tray. Then form them into cookies by pressing them with a fork. Bake for 12 to 15 minutes till they brown.

5. Take out from the oven, allowing to cool on the tray completely.

6. White Chocolate Dairy Free Peanut Butter Cups

Prep. Time: 5 minutes

Cook Time: 5 minutes

Servings: 40

The serving size is 1 cup

Nutrition as per serving:

117kcal / 6g fat / 14g carbs / 10g fiber / 3g protein = 4g net carbs

Ingredients

- White Chocolate Bar, Sugar-free, coarsely chopped 4 cups

- Peanut butter, smooth (or sunflower seed butter) 1 cup

- Coconut flour 2 tbsp.

- Unsweetened coconut milk 2 tbsp.+ more if needed

Directions

1. Line muffin liners in a standard muffin tin of 12 cups or mini muffin tin of 20 cups and put aside.

2. Removing ½ a cup of your white chocolate, melt the remaining 3 1/2 cups on the stovetop or in a microwave-safe dish, till silky and smooth. Quickly, pour the melted white chocolate equally amongst the prepared muffin cups, scrape down the sides to remove all. Once done, chill

3. Meanwhile, start making the peanut butter filling. Mix the flour and peanut butter well. Adding a tsp. of milk at a time brings to the desired texture.

4. Take the hardened white chocolate cups, then equally pour the peanut butter filling among all of them. After all, is used up, take white chocolate that was kept aside and melt them. Then pour it on each of the cups to cover fully. Chill until firm.

7. Chocolate Crunch Bars

Prep. Time: 5 minutes

Cook Time: 5 minutes

Servings: 20 servings

The serving size is 1 Bar

Nutrition as per serving:

155kcal / 12g fat / 4g carbs / 2g fiber / 7g protein = 2g net carbs

Ingredients

- Chocolate chips (stevia sweetened), 1 1/2 cups

- Almond butter (or any seed or nut butter) 1 cup

- Sticky sweetener (swerve sweetened or monk fruit syrup) 1/2 cup

- Coconut oil 1/4 cup

- Seeds and nuts (like almonds, pepitas, cashews, etc.) 3 cups

Directions

1. Line parchment paper on a baking dish of 8 x 8-inch and put it aside.

2. Combine the keto-friendly chocolate chips, coconut oil, almond butter and sticky sweetener and melt on a stovetop or a microwave-safe dish until combined.

3. Include nuts and seeds and combine until fully mixed. Pour this mixture into the parchment-lined baking dish smoothing it out with a spatula. Chill until firm.

Notes

Keep refrigerated

8. Easy Peanut Butter Cups

Prep. Time: 10minutes

Cook Time: 5minutes

Servings: 12

The serving size is 1 piece

Nutrition as per serving:

187kcal / 18g fat / 14g carbs / 11g fiber / 3g protein = 3g net carbs

Ingredients

Chocolate layers

• Dark chocolate(not bakers chocolate), Sugar-free, 10 oz. Divided

- Coconut oil 5 tbsp. (divided)

- Vanilla extracts 1/2 tsp. (divided) optional

Peanut butter layer

- Creamy Peanut butter 3 1/2 tbsp.

- Coconut oil 2 tsp.

- Powdered Erythritol (or to taste) 4 tsp.

- Peanut flour 1 1/2 tsp.

- Vanilla extracts 1/8 tsp. Optional

- Sea salt 1 pinch (or to taste) optional

Directions

1. Line parchment liners in a muffin pan

2. Prepare the chocolate layer on the stove, place a double boiler and heat half of the coconut oil and half of the chocolate, stirring regularly, until melted. (Alternatively use a microwave, heat for 20 seconds, stirring at intervals.). Add in half of the vanilla.

3. Fill each lined muffin cup with about 2 tsp. Of chocolate in each. Chill for around 10 minutes till the tops are firm.

4. Prepare the peanut butter filling: in a microwave or a double boiler, heat the coconut oil and peanut butter (similar to step 2). Mix in the peanut flour, powdered sweetener, sea salt and vanilla until smooth. Adjust salt and sweetener to taste if preferred.

5. Pour a tsp. Of the prepared peanut mixture into each cup with the chocolate layer. You don't want it to reach the edges. Chill for 10 minutes more till the tops are firm.

6. Now, prepare a chocolate layer for the top. Heat the leftover coconut oil and chocolate in a microwave or the double boiler (similar to step 2). Add in the vanilla.

7. Pour about 2 tsp of melted chocolate into each cup. It should cover the empty part and the peanut butter circles completely.

8. Again chill for at least 20 to 30 minutes, until completely solid. Keep in the refrigerator.

9. No-Bake Chocolate Coconut Bars

Prep. Time: 1 minute

Cook Time: 5 minutes

Servings: 12 bars

The serving size is 1 bar

Nutrition as per serving:

169 kcal / 17g fat / 5g carbs / 4g fiber / 2g protein = 1g net carbs

Ingredients

- Keto maple syrup 1/4 cup
- Coconut unsweetened, shredded 3 cups
- Coconut oil, melted 1 cup
- Lily's chocolate chips 1-2 cups

Directions

1. Line parchment paper in a large loaf pan or square pan and put aside.
2. Add all the ingredients to a large bowl and combine very well. Shift mixture to the prepared pan. Wet your hands lightly and press them into place. Chill for 30 minutes until firm. Cut into 12 bars.
3. Melt the sugar-free chocolate chips, and using two forks, dip each chilled bar into the melted chocolate and coat evenly. Evenly coat all the bars in the same way. Chill until chocolate solidifies.
4. Keep the Bars in a sealed container at room temperature. If you refrigerated or freeze them, thaw them completely before enjoying them.

10. Chocolate Peanut Butter Hearts

Prep. Time: 5 minutes

Cook Time: 5 minutes

Servings: 20 Hearts

The serving size is 1 Heart

Nutrition as per serving:

95kcal / 6g fat / 7g carbs / 5g fiber / 5g protein = 2g net carbs

Ingredients

- Smooth peanut butter 2 cups
- Sticky sweetener 3/4 cup
- Coconut flour 1 cup
- Chocolate chips of choice 1-2 cups

Directions

1. Line parchment paper on a large tray and put it aside.
2. Combine the keto-friendly sticky sweetener and peanut butter and melt on a stovetop or microwave-safe bowl until combined.
3. Include coconut flour and combine well. If the mixture is too thin, include more coconut flour. Leave for around 10 minutes to thicken.
4. Shape the peanut butter mixture into 18 to 20 small balls. Press each ball in. Then, using a heart-molded cookie cutter, shape the balls into hearts removing excess peanut butter mixture from the sides. Assemble the hearts on the lined tray and chill.
5. Melt the keto-friendly chocolate chips. With two forks, coat the chocolate by dipping each heart into it. Repeat with all hearts. When done, chill until firm.

Notes

Keep in a sealed jar at room temperature for up to 2 weeks, or refrigerate for up to 2 months.

11. Magic Cookies

Prep. Time: 10 minutes

Cook Time: 15 minutes

Servings: 15 cookies

The serving size is 1 cookie

Nutrition as per serving:

130kcal / 13g fat / 2g carbs / 1g fiber / 2g protein = 1g net carbs

Ingredients

- Butter softened 3 tbsp.

- Coconut oil 1/4 cup

- Granulated swerve sweetener 3 tbsp.

- Dark chocolate chips, sugar-free (like lily's) 1 cup

- Egg yolks 4 large

- Coconut flakes 1 cup

- Kosher salt 1/2 tsp.

- Walnuts roughly chopped 3/4 cup.

Directions

1. Heat oven up to 350° and line a parchment paper on a baking sheet. In a large mixing bowl, whisk together butter, coconut oil, sweetener, egg yolks and salt; stir in walnuts, coconut, and chocolate chips.

2. Drop spoonfuls of batter onto the prepared baking sheet. Place in the oven and bake for 15 mins until golden,

12. No-Bake Coconut Crack Bars

Prep. Time: 2 minutes

Cook Time: 3 minutes

Servings: 20

The serving size is 1 square

Nutrition as per serving:

108kcal / 11g fat / 2g carbs / 2g fiber /2g protein = 0g net carbs

Ingredients

• Coconut flakes unsweetened & Shredded 3 cups

• Coconut oil, melted 1 cup

• Maple syrup, monk fruit sweetened 1/4 cup (or any liquid sweetener of preference)

Directions

1. Line parchment paper on an 8 x 10-inch pan or an 8 x 8-inch pan and put aside. Or use a loaf pan.

2. Combine unsweetened shredded coconut, melted coconut oil, maple syrup (monk fruit sweetened) in a big mixing bowl and mix till you get a thick batter. If you find it crumbling, add a tsp. of water or a bit of extra syrup.

3. Transfer the coconut mixture to the lined pan. Press firmly with slightly wet hands into place. Chill until firmed. Cut into bars & enjoy!

13. Candied Pecans

Prep. Time: 5 minutes

Cook Time: 1 minute

Servings: 16 Servings

The serving size is 1 Serving

Nutrition as per serving:

139kcal / 15g fat / 3g carbs / 2g fiber / 2g protein = 1g net carbs

Ingredients

- Granulated sweetener divided 1 1/2 cups
- Vanilla extract 1 tsp
- Water 1/4 cup
- Cinnamon 1 tbsp.
- Raw pecans 3 cups

Directions

1. Over medium flame, heat a skillet or large pan.
2. Add 1 cup of the granulated sweetener, vanilla extract and water, and stir until fully mixed. Let it heat up, stirring in between.
3. Once the sweetener is fully melted, include your pecans. Stir around the pecans ensuring every nut is equally coated in the liquid mixture. Keep occasionally stirring till the sweetener starts to set on the pecans. Take off from the heat. Leave for 2 to 3 minutes.
4. Brea apart the pecans with a wooden spoon before they set together.
5. When cooled, mix with the granulated sweetener that was reserved earlier and cinnamon. Store in a sealed container.

14. Sugar-Free Flourless Cookies

Prep. Time: 2 minutes

Cook Time: 10 minutes

Servings: 14 cookies

The serving size is 1 Cookie

Nutrition as per serving:

101kcal / 9g fat / 3g carbs / 1g fiber / 5g protein = 3g net carbs

Ingredients

For the original style:

- Almond butter 1 cup
- Egg 1 large
- Granulated sweetener, stevia blend monk fruit, 3 /4 cup

For the egg-free style:

- Almond butter smooth 1 cup
- Chia seeds, ground 3-4 tbsp.
- Granulated sweetener, stevia blend monk fruit 3/4 cup

Directions

1. Heat the oven up to 350 degrees. Place parchment paper on a cookie sheet or a baking tray.
2. In a big mixing bowl, add all the ingredients and blend until well combined. When using the egg-free recipe, begin with 3 tbsps. of grounded chia seeds. Add an extra tbsp. if the mixture is still too thin.

3. Using your hands or a cookie scoop, shape small balls and place them 3 to 4 inches apart on the baking tray. Make into cookie shape by pressing down with a fork. Bake until cookies are beginning to get a golden brown color but still soft, or for 8 to 10 minutes. Take out from the oven, allowing to cool until firm but soft and chewy.

15. Salted Caramel Fudge

Prep. Time: 5 minutes

Cook Time: 5 minutes

Servings: 24 servings

The serving size is 1 fudge cup

Nutrition as per serving:

148kcal / 15g fat / 4g carbs / 2g fiber / 4g protein = 2g net carbs

Ingredients

- Cashew butter 2 cups
- Keto maple syrup 1/4 cup
- Coconut oil 1/2 cup

Directions

1. Line muffin liners in a mini muffin tin of 24-count and put aside.
2. Combine all the ingredients on a stovetop or in a microwave-safe dish and heat till melted.
3. Take off from heat and beat very well till a glossy, smooth texture remains.
4. Split the fudge mixture equally in the lined muffin tin. Chill for about 30 minutes, till firm.

16. Healthy Kit Kat Bars

Prep. Time: 5 minutes

Cook Time: 5 minutes

Servings: 20 Bars

The serving size is 1 Bar

Nutrition as per serving:

149kcal / 12g fat / 4g carbs / 2g fiber / 7g protein = 2g net carbs

Ingredients

- Keto granola 2 cups
- Almond butter (or any seed or nut butter) 1 cup
- Mixed seeds 1/2 cup
- Coconut oil 1/4 cup
- Mixed nuts 1/2 cup
- Dark chocolate chips, 1 1/2 cups
- Sticky sweetener 1/2 cup

Directions

1. Mix the mixed nuts, keto granola, and seeds in a big bowl. Put aside.
2. Melt the keto chocolate chips on the stovetop or in a microwave-safe dish. Include almond butter, coconut oil, and sticky sweetener. Heat until well combined.
3. Add the melted chocolate mixture onto the dry and combine until fully unified.
4. Shift the kit kat mixture to a pan of 10 x 10-inch lined with parchment. With a spatula, smooth out to a uniform layer. Chill for about 30 minutes, then slice into bars.

Notes: keep refrigerated

17. Healthy No-Bake Keto Cookie Bars

Prep. Time: 5 minutes

Cook Time: 25 minutes

Servings: 12 servings

The serving size is 1 Bar

Nutrition as per serving:

149kcal / 5g fat / 10g carbs / 6g fiber / 10g protein = 4g net carbs

Ingredients

For the cookie

- Almond flour blanched 1 1/2 cups

- Coconut flour 1/4 cup

- Cinnamon, a pinch

- Protein powder, vanilla flavor (optional) 2 scoops

- Granulated sweetener (like

- Sticky sweetener, keto-friendly, 1/2 cup

- Monk fruit sweetener) 2 tbsp.

- Vanilla extract 1/2 tsp

- Cashew butter (or any nut butter) 1/2 cup

- Sticky sweetener, keto-friendly, 1/2 cup

- Almond milk 1 tbsp.

For the protein icing

- Protein powder,

- Vanilla flavor 3 scoops

- Granulated sweetener, keto-friendly 1-2 tbsp. + for sprinkling 1/2 tsp

- Almond milk, (for batter) 1 tbsp.

For the coconut butter icing

- Coconut butter melted 4-6 tbsp.

- Sticky sweetener, 2 tbsp.

- Almond milk 1 tbsp.

Directions

1. Preparing sugar cookie base

2. Place tin foil in a baking pan of 8 x 8 inches and put aside.

3. Mix the protein powder, flours, granulated sweetener and cinnamon in a big mixing bowl, and put aside.

4. Melt the sticky sweetener with cashew butter on a stovetop or a microwave-proof bowl. Stir in the vanilla extract and add to the dry mixture. Beat superbly until fully combined. If the batter formed is too thick, add a tablespoon of almond milk with a tablespoon and mix well until desired consistency.

5. Pour the batter into the lined baking sheet and press tightly in place. Scatter the ½ teaspoon of keto-friendly granulated sweetener and chill for about 15 minutes until they are firm. Then add an icing of choice and chill for 30 minutes more to settle the icing before slicing.

6. Preparing the icing(s)

7. Mix all ingredients of the icings (separately) and, using almond milk, thin down the mixture till a very thick icing is formed.

18. Keto Chocolate Bark with Almonds and Bacon

Prep. Time: 30 minutes

Servings: 8 servings

The serving size is 1/8 of the recipe

Nutrition as per serving:

157kcal /12.8g fat / 4g protein / 7.5g fiber / 12.7g carbs = 5.2g net carbs

Ingredients

• Sugar-free Chocolate Chips 1 bag (9 oz.)

• Chopped Almonds 1/2 cup

• Bacon cooked & crumbled 2 slices

Directions

1. In a microwave-safe bowl, melt the chocolate chips on high in 30 seconds intervals, stirring every time until all chocolate is melted.

2. Include the chopped almonds into the melted chocolate and mix.

3. Line a baking sheet with parchment and pour the chocolate mixture on it in a thin layer of about 1/2 inch.

4. Immediately top the chocolate with the crumbled bacon and press in with a flat spoon.

5. Chill for around 20 minutes or till the chocolate has solidified. Peel the parchment away from the hardened chocolate and crack it into eight pieces. Keep refrigerated.

Chapter 2- Chaffles

1. Basic chaffle recipe

Prep. Time: 5 minutes

Cook Time: 5 minutes

Servings: 1 chaffle

The serving size is 1 chaffle

Nutrition as per serving:

291kcal / 23g fat / 1g carbs / 0g fiber / 20g protein = 1g net carbs

Ingredients

• Sharp cheddar cheese shredded 1/2 cup

• Eggs 1

Directions

1. Whisk the egg.

2. In the waffle maker, assemble 1/4 cup of shredded cheese.

3. Top the cheese with beaten egg.

4. Top with the remainder 1/4 cup of cheese.

5. Cook till it's golden and crispy. It will get crispier as it cools.

2. Keto Oreo Chaffles

Prep. Time: 15 minutes

Cook Time: 8 minutes

Servings: 2 full-size chaffles or 4 mini chaffles

The serving size is 2 chaffles

Nutrition as per serving:

381kcal / 14.6g fat / 14g carbs / 5g fiber / 17g protein = 9g net carbs

Ingredients

- Sugar-Free Chocolate Chips 1/2 cup

- Butter 1/2 cup

- Eggs 3

- Truvia 1/4 cup

- Vanilla extract 1tsp.

- For Cream Cheese Frosting

- Butter, room temperature 4 oz.

- Cream Cheese, room temperature 4 oz.

- Powdered Swerve 1/2 cup

- Heavy Whipping Cream 1/4 cup

- Vanilla extract 1tsp.

Directions

1. Melt the butter and chocolate for around 1 minute in a microwave-proof dish. Stir well. You really ought to use the warmth within the chocolate and butter to melt most of the clumps. You have overheated the chocolate; when you microwave, and all is melted, it means you have overheated the chocolate. So grab yourself a spoon and begin stirring. If required, add 10 seconds, but stir just before you plan to do so.

2. Put the eggs, vanilla and sweetener, in a bowl and whisk until fluffy and light.

3. In a steady stream, add the melted chocolate into the egg mix and whisk again until well-combined.

4. In a Waffle Maker, pour around 1/4 of the mixture and cook for 7 to-8 minutes until it's crispy.

5. Prepare the frosting as they are cooking.

6. Put all the frosting ingredients into a food processor bowl and mix until fluffy and smooth. To achieve the right consistency, include a little extra cream.

7. To create your Oreo Chaffle, spread or pipe the frosting evenly in between the two chaffles.

8. The waffle machine, do not overfill it! It will create a giant mess and ruin the batter and the maker, utilizing no more than 1/4 cup of the batter.

9. Leave the waffles to cool down a bit before frosting. It is going to help them to remain crisp.

10. To make the frosting, use room-temp butter and cream cheese.

3. Glazed Donut Chaffle

Prep. Time: 10 mins

Cook Time: 5 mins

Servings: 3 chaffles

The serving size is 1 chaffle

Nutrition as per serving:

312kcal / 15g fat / 6g carbs / 1g fiber / 9g protein = 5g net carbs

Ingredients

For the chaffles

• Mozzarella cheese shredded ½ cup

• Whey protein isolates Unflavored 2 tbsp.

• Cream Cheese 1 oz.

- Swerve confectioners (Sugar substitute) 2 tbsp.

- Vanilla extract ½tsp.

- Egg 1

- Baking powder ½tsp.

For the glaze topping:

- Heavy whipping cream2 tbsp.

- Swerve confectioners (sugar substitute) 3-4 tbsp.

- Vanilla extract ½tsp.

Directions

1. Turn on the waffle maker.

2. In a microwave-proof bowl, combine the cream cheese and mozzarella cheese. Microwave at 30-second breaks until it is all melted and stir to combine completely.

3. Include the whey protein, baking powder, 2 tbsp. Keto sweetener to the melted cheese, and work with your hands to knead until well combined.

4. Put the dough in a mixing bowl, and whisk in the vanilla and egg into it to form a smooth batter.

5. Put 1/3 of the mixture into the waffle machine, and let it cook for 3 to 5 minutes.

6. Repeat the above step 5 to make a total of three chaffles.

7. Whisk the glaze topping ingredients together and drizzle on top of the chaffles generously before serving.

4. Keto Pumpkin Chaffles

Prep. Time: 2 mins

Cook Time: 5 mins

Servings: 2 chaffles

The serving size is 2 chaffles

Nutrition as per serving: (without toppings)

250kcal / 15g fat / 5g carbs / 1g fiber / 23g protein = 4g net carbs

Ingredients

- Mozzarella cheese, shredded ½ cup

- Egg, beaten 1 whole

- Pumpkin purée 1 ½ tbsp.

- Swerve confectioners ½tsp.

- Vanilla extract ½tsp.

- Pumpkin pie spice ¼tsp.

- Pure maple extract ⅛tsp.

- For topping- optional

- roasted pecans, cinnamon, whip cream and sugar-free maple syrup

Directions

1. Switch on the Waffle Maker and begin preparing the mixture.

2. Add all the given ingredients to a bowl, except for the mozzarella cheese, and whisk. Include the cheese and combine until well mixed.

3. Grease the waffle plates and put half the mixture into the middle of the plate. Cover the lid for 4- to 6 minutes, based on how crispy Chaffles you like.

4. Take it out and cook the second one. Serve with all or some mix of toppings, like sugar-free maple syrup, butter, roasted pecans, and a dollop of whipping cream or ground cinnamon dust.

5. Cream Cheese Chaffle with Lemon Curd

Prep. Time: 5 minutes

Cook Time: 4 minutes

Additional Time: 40 minute

Servings: 2-3 serving

The serving size is 1 chaffle

Nutrition as per serving:

302 kcals / 24g fat / 6g carbs / 1g fiber / 15g protein = 5g net carbs

Ingredients

- One batch keto lemon curd (recipe here)

- Eggs 3 large

- Cream cheese softened 4 oz.

- Lakanto monkfruit (or any low carb sweetener) 1 tbsp.

- Vanilla extract 1tsp.

- Mozzarella cheese shredded 3/4 cup

- Coconut flour 3 tbsp.

- Baking powder 1tsp.

- Salt 1/3tsp.

- Homemade keto whipped cream (optional) (recipe here)

Directions

1. Prepare lemon curd according to Directions and let cool in the refrigerator.

2. Turn on the waffle maker and grease it with oil.

3. Take a small bowl, put coconut flour, salt and baking powder. Combine and put aside.

4. Take a large bowl, put cream cheese, eggs, vanilla and sweetener. With an electric beater, beat until foamy. You may see chunks of cream cheese, and that is okay.

5. Include mozzarella cheese into the egg mixture and keep beating.

6. Pour the dry ingredients into the egg mixture and keep mixing until well blended.

7. Put batter into the preheated waffle machine and cook.

8. Take off from waffle machine; spread cooled lemon curd, top with keto whipped cream and enjoy.

6. Strawberries & Cream Keto Chaffles

Prep. Time: 25 minutes

Cook Time: 10 minutes

Servings: 8 chaffles

The serving size is 1 chaffle

Nutrition as per serving:

328cals / 12g fat / 8g carbs / 4g fiber / 6g protein = 4g net carbs

Ingredients

- Cream cheese 3 oz.

- Mozzarella cheese, shredded 2 cups

- Eggs, beaten 2

- Almond flour 1/2 cup

- Swerve confectioner sweetener 3 tbsp. + 1 tbsp.

- Baking powder 2tsps

- Strawberries 8

- Whipped cream 1 cup (canister - 2 tbsp. Per waffle)

Directions

1. In a microwavable dish, add the mozzarella and cream cheese, cook for 1 minute, mixing well. If the cheese is all melted, then go to the next step. Else cook for another 30 seconds stirring well.

2. Take another bowl, whisk eggs, including the almond flour, 3 tbsp. of keto sweetener, and baking powder.

3. Include the melted cheese mixture into the egg and almond flour mixture and combine well. Carefully add in 2 strawberries coarsely chopped. Chill for 20 minutes.

4. Meanwhile, slice the unused strawberries and mix with 1 tbsp. of Swerve. Chill.

5. Take out the batter from the refrigerator after 20 minutes. Heat the waffle iron and grease it.

6. Put 1/4 cup of the batter in the mid of the heated waffle iron. Ensuring the waffles are small makes it easier to remove from the waffle maker.

7. Transfer to a plate when cooked and cool before adding whipped cream and topping with strawberries.

This recipe gave me eight small waffles.

7. Keto Peanut Butter Cup Chaffle

Prep. Time: 2 minutes

Cook Time: 5 minutes

Servings: 2 Chaffles

The serving size is 1 chaffle + filling

Nutrition as per serving:

264kcal / 21.6g fat / 7.2g carbs / 2g fiber / 9.45g protein = 4.2g net carbs

Ingredients

For the Chaffle

- Heavy Cream 1 tbsp.
- Vanilla Extract 1/2 tsp
- Egg 1
- Cake Batter Flavor 1/2 tsp
- Unsweetened Cocoa 1 tbsp.
- Coconut Flour 1 tsp
- Lakanto Powdered Sweetener 1 tbsp.
- Baking Powder 1/4 tsp

For Peanut Butter Filling

- Heavy Cream 2 tbsp.
- All-natural Peanut Butter 3 tbsp.
- Lakanto Powdered Sweetener 2 tsp

Directions

1. Preheat a waffle maker.
2. Combine all the chaffle ingredients in a small mixing bowl.
3. Put half of the chaffle batter into the middle of the waffle machine and cook for 3 to 5 minutes.
4. Cautiously remove and duplicate for the second chaffle. Leave chaffles for a couple of minutes to let them crisp up.
5. Prepare the peanut butter filling by blending all the ingredients together and layer between chaffles.

8. Vanilla Chocolate Chip

Prep. Time: 1 minute

Cook Time: 4 minutes

Servings: 1 serving

The serving size is 1 large or 2 mini chaffle

Nutrition as per serving:

297.6 kcal. / 20.1g fat / 5.2g carbs / 1.5g fiber / 22.2g protein = 3.9g net carbs

Ingredients

- Mozzarella shredded 1/2 cup
- Eggs 1 medium
- Granulated sweetener keto 1 tbsp.
- Vanilla extract 1 tsp
- Almond meal or flour 2 tbsp.
- Chocolate chips, sugar-free 1 tbsp.

Directions

1. Mix all the ingredients in a large bowl.
2. Turn on the waffle maker. When it is heated, grease with olive oil and put half the mixture into the waffle machine. Cook for 2 to 4 minutes, then take out and repeat. It will make 2 small-chaffles per recipe.
3. Enjoy with your favorite toppings.

9. Chaffle Churro

Prep. Time: 10 minutes

Cook Time: 6-10 minutes

Servings: 2

The serving size is 4 churros

Nutrition as per serving:

189 kcals / 14.3g fat / 5.g carbs / 1g fiber / 10g protein = 4g net carbs

Ingredients

- Egg 1
- Almond flour 1 Tbsp.
- Vanilla extract ½ tsp.
- Cinnamon divided 1 tsp.
- Baking powder ¼ tsp.
- Shredded mozzarella ½ cup.
- Swerve confectioners (or any sugar substitute) 1 Tbsp.
- Swerve brown sugar (keto-friendly sugar substitute) 1 Tbsp.
- Butter melted 1 Tbsp.

Directions

1. Heat the waffle iron.
2. Combine the almond flour, egg, vanilla extract, baking powder, ½ tsp of cinnamon, swerve confectioners' sugar and shredded mozzarella in a bowl, and stir to combine well.
3. Spread half of the batter equally onto the waffle iron, and let it cook for 3 to 5 minutes. Cooking for more time will give a crispier chaffle.
4. Take out the cooked chaffle and pour the remaining batter onto it. Close the lid and cook for about 3 to 5 minutes.
5. Make both the chaffles into strips.
6. Put the cut strips in a bowl and drizzle on melted butter generously.
7. In another bowl, stir together the keto brown sugar and the leftover ½ tsp of cinnamon until well-combined.
8. Toss the churro chaffle strips in the sugar-cinnamon mixture in the bowl to coat them evenly.

10. Keto Cauliflower Chaffles Recipe

Prep. Time: 5 minutes

Cook Time: 4 minutes

Servings: 2 chaffles

The serving size is 2 chaffles

Nutrition as per serving:

246kcal / 16g fat / 7g carbs / 2g fiber / 20g protein = 5g net carbs

Ingredients

- Riced cauliflower 1 cup
- Garlic powder 1/4tsp.
- Ground black pepper 1/4tsp.
- Italian seasoning 1/2tsp.
- Kosher salt 1/4tsp.
- Mozzarella cheese shredded 1/2 cup
- Eggs 1
- Parmesan cheese shredded 1/2 cup

Directions

1. In a blender, add all the ingredients and blend well. Turn the waffle maker on.
2. Put 1/8 cup of parmesan cheese onto the waffle machine. Ensure to cover up the bottom of the waffle machine entirely.
3. Cover the cheese with the cauliflower batter, then sprinkle another layer of parmesan cheese on the cauliflower mixture. Cover and cook.
4. Cook for 4 to 5 minutes, or till crispy.
5. Will make 2 regular-size chaffles or 4 mini chaffles.
6. It freezes well. Prepare a big lot and freeze for the future.

11. Zucchini Chaffles

Prep. Time: 10 minutes

Cook Time: 5 minutes

Servings: 2 chaffles

The serving size is 1 chaffle

Nutrition as per serving:

194kcal / 13g fat / 4g carbs / 1g fiber / 16g protein = 3g net carbs

Ingredients

- Zucchini, grated 1 cup

- Eggs, beaten 1

- Parmesan cheese shredded 1/2 cup

- Mozzarella cheese shredded 1/4 cup

- Dried basil, 1tsp. Or fresh basil, chopped 1/4 cup

- Kosher Salt, divided 3/4tsp.

- Ground Black Pepper 1/2tsp.

Directions

1. Put the shredded zucchini in a bowl and Sprinkle salt, about 1/4tsp on it and leave it aside to gather other ingredients. Moments before using put the zucchini in a paper towel, wrap and press to wring out all the extra water.

2. Take a bowl and whisk in the egg. Include the mozzarella, grated zucchini, basil, and pepper 1/2tsp of salt.

3. Cover the waffle maker base with a layer of 1 to 2 tbsp. of the shredded parmesan.

4. Then spread 1/4 of the zucchini batter. Spread another layer of 1 to 2 tbsp. of shredded parmesan and shut the lid.

5. Let it cook for 4 to 8 minutes. It depends on the dimensions of your waffle machine. Normally, once the chaffle is not emitting vapors of steam, it is nearly done. For the greatest results, let it cook until good and browned.

6. Take out and duplicate for the next waffle.

Will make 4 small chaffles or 2 full-size chaffles in a Mini waffle maker.

12. Keto Pizza Chaffle

Prep. Time: 10 minutes

Cook Time: 30 minutes

Servings: 2 servings

The serving size is 1 chaffle

Nutrition as per serving:

76 kcal / 4.3g fat / 4.1g carbs / 1.2g fiber / 5.5g protein = 3.2g net carbs

Ingredients

- Egg 1

- Mozzarella cheese shredded 1/2 cup

- Italian seasoning a pinch

- Pizza sauce No sugar added 1 tbsp.

- Toppings – pepperoni, shredded cheese (or any other toppings)

Directions

- Heat the waffle maker.

- Whisk the egg, and Italian seasonings in a small mixing bowl, together.

- Stir in the cheese, leaving a few tsps. for layering.

- Layer a tsp of grated cheese onto the preheated waffle machine and allow it to cook for about 30 seconds.

- It will make a crispier crust.

- Pour half the pizza mixture into the waffle maker and allow to cook for around 4 minutes till it's slightly crispy and golden brown!

- Take out the waffle and make the second chaffle with the remaining mixture.

- Spread the pizza sauce, pepperoni and shredded cheese. Place in Microwave and heat on high for around 20 seconds and done! On the spot Chaffle PIZZA!

13. Crispy Taco Chaffle Shells

Prep. Time: 5 minutes

Cook Time: 8 minutes

Servings: 2 chaffles

The serving size is 1 chaffle

Nutrition as per serving:

258kcal / 19g fat / 4g carbs / 2g fiber / 18g protein = 2g net carbs

Ingredients

- Egg white 1

- Monterey jack cheese shredded 1/4 cup
- Sharp cheddar cheese shredded 1/4 cup
- Water 3/4 tsp
- Coconut flour 1 tsp
- Baking powder 1/4 tsp
- Chili powder 1/8 tsp
- Salt a pinch

Directions

1. Turn on the Waffle iron and lightly grease it with oil when it is hot.

2. In a mixing bowl, mix all of the above ingredients and blend to combine.

3. Pour half of the mixture onto the waffle iron and shut the lid. Cook for 4 minutes without lifting the lid. The chaffle will not set in less than 4 minutes.

4. Take out the cooked taco chaffle and put it aside. Do the same process with the remaining chaffle batter.

5. Put a muffin pan upside down and assemble the taco chaffle upon the cups to make into a taco shell. Put aside for a few minutes.

6. When it is firm, fill it with your favorite Taco Meat fillings. Serve.

Enjoy this delicious keto crispy taco chaffle shell with your favorite toppings.

Chapter 3- Keto Cakes and Cupcakes

1. Chocolate Cake with Chocolate Icing

Prep. Time: 10 minutes

Cook Time: 25 minutes

Servings: 9 slices

The serving size is 1 slice

Nutrition as per serving:

358kcal / 33g fat / 11g carbs / 6g fiber / 8g protein = 5g net carbs

Ingredients

- Coconut flour 3/4 cup
- Granular sweetener 3/4 cup
- Cocoa powder 1/2 cup
- Baking powder 2tsps
- Eggs 6
- Heavy whipping cream 2/3 cup
- Melted butter 1/2 cup
- For chocolate icing
- Heavy whipping cream 1 cup
- Keto granular sweetener 1/4 cup
- Vanilla extracts 1tsp.
- Cocoa powder sifted 1/3 cup

Directions

1. Heat the oven up to 350F.
2. Oil a cake pan of 8x8.
3. In a large mixing bowl, put all the cake ingredients to blend well with an electric mixer or a stand mixer.
4. Transfer the batter to the oiled pan and put in the heated oven for 25 minutes or till a toothpick inserted in the center comes out clean.
5. Take out from the oven. Leave to cool fully before icing.
6. Prepare the Icing
7. With an electric mixer, beat the whipping cream until stiff peaks form. Include the cocoa powder, swerve, and vanilla. Keep beating until just combined.
8. Spread the icing evenly all over the cake and serve. Keep any remains in the refrigerator.

2. 4 Ingredients Cheesecake Fluff

Prep. Time: 10 minutes

Servings: 6

The serving size is ½ cup

Nutrition as per serving:

258kcal / 27g fat / 4g carbs / 0g fiber / 4g protein = 4g net carbs

Ingredients

- Heavy Whipping Cream1 Cup
- Cream Cheese, Softened 1 Brick (8 oz.)
- Lemon Zest 1 tsp.
- Keto-friendly Granular Sweetener 1/2 Cup

Directions

1. Prepare the Fluff
2. Put the heavy cream in a bowl of a stand mixer and beat until stiff peaks begin to form. An electric beater or a hand beater can also be used.
3. Transfer the whipped cream into a separate bowl and put aside
4. To the same stand mixer bowl, add the cream cheese (softened), sweetener, zest, and whisk until smooth.
5. Now add the whipped cream to the cream cheese into the mixer bowl. Fold with a spatula gently till it is halfway combined. Finish whipping with the stand mixer until smooth.
6. Top with your fave toppings and serve.

3. Mug Cake Peanut Butter, Chocolate or Vanilla

Prep. Time: 4 minutes

Cook Time: 1 minute

Servings: 1

The serving size is 1 mug cake

Nutrition as per serving:

(For mug cake with almond flour: chocolate flavor and no chocolate chips)

312 kcal / 7 carbs/ 28g fat / 12g protein/4g fiber = 3 net carbs

(Peanut butter flavor and no chocolate chips)

395 kcal / 8 carbs /35g fat / 15g protein/4g fiber = 5 net carb

(Vanilla flavor and no chocolate chips)

303 kcal / 5 carbs/ 28g fat / 11g protein /2g fiber = 3 net carb

Ingredients

- Butter melted 1 Tbsp.

- Almond flour 3 Tbsp. or Coconut flour 1 Tbsp.

- Granular Sweetener 2 Tbsp.

- Sugar-free Peanut butter 1 Tbsp. (For Peanut Butter flavor)

- Cocoa powder 1 Tbsp. (For Chocolate flavor)

- Baking powder ½ tsp.

- Egg, beaten 1

- Sugar-free Chocolate Chips 1 Tbsp.

- Vanilla few drops

Directions

For Vanilla flavor

1. In a microwave-proof coffee mug, heat the butter for 10 seconds to melt in the microwave.
2. Include the almond flour or coconut flour, baking powder, sweetener, beaten egg and vanilla. Combine well.
3. For 60 seconds, microwave on high, ensuring not to overcook; otherwise, it will come out dry. Sprinkle keto chocolate chips on top if preferred or stir in before cooking.

For Chocolate flavor

In a microwave-proof coffee mug, heat the butter for 10 seconds to melt in the microwave. Include the almond flour or coconut flour, cocoa powder, sweetener, baking powder, beaten egg and vanilla. Combine well. For 60 seconds, microwave on high, ensuring not to overcook; it will come out dry. Sprinkle keto chocolate chips on top if preferred.

For Peanut Butter flavor

1. In a microwave-proof coffee mug, heat the butter for 10 seconds to melt in the microwave.

2. Include the almond flour or coconut flour, baking powder, sweetener, beaten egg and vanilla. Combine well. Stir in peanut butter. For 60 seconds, microwave on high, ensuring not to overcook; otherwise, it will come out dry. Sprinkle keto chocolate chips on top if preferred.

Directions for Baking: Bake in an oven-safe small bowl. Bake in the oven for 15 to 20 minutes at 350.

4. Chocolate Coconut Flour Cupcakes

Prep. Time: 10 minutes

Cook Time: 25 minutes

Servings: 12 cupcakes

The serving size is 1 cupcake

Nutrition as per serving:

268 kcal / 22g fat / 6g carbs / 3g fiber / 6g protein = 3g net carbs

Ingredients

For Cupcakes:

• Butter melted 1/2 cup

• Cocoa powder 7 tbsp.

• Instant coffee granules 1 tsp (optional)

• Eggs at room temperature 7

• Vanilla extracts 1 tsp

• Coconut flour 2/3 cup

• Baking powder 2 tsp

• Swerve sweetener 2/3 cup

- Salt 1/2 tsp

- Hemp milk or unsweetened almond milk 1/2 cup (+more)

For Espresso Buttercream:

- Hot water 2 tbsp.

- Instant coffee or instant espresso powder 2 tsp

- Whipping cream 1/2 cup

- Butter softened 6 tbsp.

- Cream cheese softened 4 oz.

- Swerve powdered sweetener 1/2 cup

Directions

For Cupcakes:

1. Heat the oven up to 350F and line silicone liners or parchment on a muffin tin.

2. Mix together the cocoa powder, melted butter, and espresso powder in a large mixing bowl,

3. Include the vanilla and eggs and whisk until well combined. Now add in the coconut flour, baking powder, salt and sweetener, and mix until smooth.

4. Pour the almond milk in and stir. If the batter is very thick, add in 1 tbsp. of almond milk at a time to thin it out. It should not be pourable but of scoopable consistency.

5. Scoop the batter equally among the prepared muffin tins and put in the oven's center rack, baking for 20-25 minutes. Check the cupcakes with a tester inserted into the center comes out clean, then cupcakes are done. Leave to cool in the pan for 5 to 10 minutes, and then cool completely on a wire rack.

For Buttercream:

1. Dissolve the coffee in hot water. Put aside.

2. Whip cream using an electric mixer until stiff peaks are formed. Put aside.

3. Beat cream cheese, butter, and sweetener all together in a medium mixing bowl until creamy. Include coffee mixture and mix until combined. fold in the whipped cream Using a rubber spatula carefully till well combined.

4. Layer frosting on the cooled cupcakes with an offset spatula or a knife.

5. Low-carb red velvet cupcakes/ cake

Prep. Time: 15-30 minutes

Cook Time: 20-25 minutes

Servings: 12 slice

The serving size is 1 slice

Nutrition as per serving:

193kcals / 12g fat / 6.4g carbs / 1g fiber / 5.9g protein = 5.4g net carbs

Ingredients

- Almond flour 1+ 3/4 cups

- Swerve confectioner sweetener (not substitutes) 2/3 cup

- Cocoa powder 2 tbsp.

- Baking powder 2tsp.

- Baking soda 1/2tsp.

- Eggs 2

- Full fat coconut milk 1/2 cup + 2 tbsp.

- Olive oil 3 tbsp.

- Apple cider vinegar 1 tbsp.

- Vanilla extract 1 tbsp.

- Red food coloring 2 tbsp.

For frosting

- Cream cheese at room temperature 1 container (8 oz.)

- Butter softened 2 ½ tbsp.

- Swerve confectioner sweetener 1 cup

- Coconut milk 2 ½ tbsp.

- Vanilla extract 1tsp.

- Salt 1/8tsp.

**Double Frosting for Layer Cake

Directions

1. Preheat oven to 350 degrees

2. In a large mixing bowl, add the wet ingredients, eggs, milk, vanilla extract, olive oil, apple cider vinegar and food coloring. Blend until smooth.

3. Now sift together the cocoa powder, Swerve Confectioner, baking powder and baking soda, add to the wet ingredients, and incorporate it into the batter with an electric mixer or a hand whisk.

4. Lastly, sift in the almond flour. Moving the flour back and forth with a whisk will speed up the process significantly. Fold the sifted flour gently into the batter till smooth and all is well incorporated. Use the batter immediately.

5. To make Cupcakes: Scoop batter into the muffin liners, fill only up to 2/3 of liner -do not over-fill. Ensure the oven is heated, put in the oven for 15 minutes at 350 degrees, and then turn the muffin tin in 180 degrees and cook for an extra 10 minutes. (Bear in mind, oven times vary occasionally - humidity and altitude can impact things, so watch closely as they may need a few minutes more or even less).

6. Take out from the oven, do not remove from pan and set aside to cool completely.

7. For Layer Cake: 2 Layer- line parchment paper in two cake pans (8 inches each) and oil the sides. Transfer batter to both pans evenly. Use a wet spatula to spread the batter smoothly. Apply the same process for three layers, but using thinner pans as dividing the batter three ways-every layers will become thin.

8. Place pans into oven for 20-25 minutes baking at 350 degrees. Cautiously turn the pans 180 degrees halfway through baking and cover lightly with a foil. At 20 to 25 minutes, take out the pans; they will be a bit soft. Set them aside to cool completely. When they are cool, take a knife and run it around the side of the pan and turn them over carefully onto a plate or cooling rack and leave them for an extra 5 to 10 minutes before icing.

9. Meanwhile, prepare. Blend the softened butter and cream cheese together With an electric beater. Include milk and vanilla extract and beat again. Lastly, sift in the Swerve, salt mixing well one last time. If you want a thicker frosting, chill it in the refrigerator. Or adding more Swerve will give a thicker texture or add more milk to make it thinner. * For a layer cake, double the frosting recipe.

10. Spread or pipe frosting onto cupcakes, sprinkle some decoration if desired and enjoy!! To frost layer cake, it is simpler to first chill the layers in the freezer. Then frost and pile each layer to end frost the sides and top.

Keep any leftovers in a sealed box and refrigerate. Enjoy!

6. Vanilla Cupcakes

Prep. Time: 5 minutes

Cook Time: 20 minutes

Servings: 10 Cupcakes

The serving size is 1 cupcake

Nutrition as per serving:

153kcal / 13g fat / 4g carbs / 2g fiber / 5g protein = 2g net carbs

Ingredients

- Butter 1/2 cup
- Keto granulated sweetener 2/3 cup
- Vanilla extract 2 tsp
- Eggs whisked * See notes 6 large
- Milk of choice ** See notes 2 tbsp.
- Coconut flour 1/2 cup
- Baking powder 1 tsp
- Keto vanilla frosting 1 batch

Directions

1. Heat the oven up to 350F/180C. Place muffin liners in a 12-cup muffin tin and oil 10 of them.
2. Beat the butter, salt, sugar, eggs and vanilla extract together in a big mixing bowl when combined-well include the milk and mix until blended.
3. In another bowl, sift the baking powder and coconut flour together. Add the wet ingredients to the dry and mix until combined.
4. Pour the batter equally into the ten muffin cups, filling up to ¾ full. Place the cupcakes on the middle rack and bake for 17 to 20 minutes until the muffin top springs back to touch

5. Remove the muffin pan from the oven, set it aside to cool for 10 minutes, and then cool completely on a wire rack. Frost, when cooled.

7. Healthy Flourless Fudge Brownies

Prep. Time: 5 minutes

Cook Time: 20 minutes

Servings: 12 servings

The serving size is 1 Brownie

Nutrition as per serving:

86kcal / 5g fat / 5g carbs / 3g fiber / 7g protein = 2g net carbs

Ingredients

- Pumpkin puree 2 cups
- Almond butter 1 cup
- Cocoa powder 1/2 cup
- Granulated sweetener (or liquid stevia drops) 1/4 cup

For the Chocolate Coconut Frosting

- Chocolate chips 2 cups
- Coconut milk canned 1 cup
- For the chocolate protein frosting
- Protein powder, chocolate flavor 2 scoops
- Granulated sweetener 1-2 tbsp.
- Seed or nut butter of choice 1-2 tbsp.
- Milk or liquid *1 tbsp.

For the Cheese Cream Frosting

- Cream cheese 125 grams
- Cocoa powder 1-2 tbsp.

- Granulated sweetener of choice 1-2 tbsp.

Directions

1. For the fudge brownies

2. Heat the oven up to 350 degrees, oil a loaf pan or small cake pan and put aside.

3. Melt the nut butter in a small microwave-proof bowl. In a big mixing bowl, put in the pumpkin puree, dark cocoa powder, nut butter, and combine very well.

4. Transfer the mixture to the oiled pan and put in preheated oven for around 20 to 25 minutes or until fully baked. Remove from the oven, set aside to cool completely. When cooled, apply the frosting and chill for about 30 minutes to settle.

Preparing the cream cheese or protein frosting:

1. In a big mixing bowl, mix together all the ingredients and beat well. With a tablespoon. keep adding dairy-free milk till a frosting consistency is reached.

2. For the coconut chocolate ganache

3. In a microwave-proof bowl, combine all the ingredients and heat gradually until just mixed- whisk till a glossy and thick frosting remains.

8. Healthy Keto Chocolate Raspberry Mug Cake

Prep. Time: 1 minute

Cook Time: 1 minute

Servings: 1 serving

The serving size is 1 mug cake

Nutrition as per serving:

152kcal / 8g fat / 13g carbs / 8g fiber / 7g protein = 5g net carbs

Ingredients

- Coconut flour 1 tbsp.

- Granulated sweetener of choice 1 tbsp.

- Cocoa powder 2 tbsp.

- Baking powder 1/4 tsp

- Sunflower seed butter (or any seed or nut butter) 1 tbsp.

- Pumpkin puree 3 tbsp.

- Frozen or fresh raspberries 1/4 cup

- Coconut milk unsweetened 1-2 tbsp.

Directions

1. In a microwave-proof mug, put in the dry ingredients and stir well.

2. Add in the rest of the ingredients, except for milk and raspberries, and combine until a thick batter is formed.

3. Stir in the raspberries and add one tbsp. of milk. Add extra milk if the batter gets too thick. Place in microwave and cook for 1 to 2 minutes. Should come out gooey in the center. If you overcook, it will become dry.

Oven Directions

1. Heat oven up to 180C.

2. Oil an oven-proof ramekin. Add the prepared batter and put in the oven for 10-12 minutes, or until done.

9. Keto Avocado Brownies

Prep. Time: 10 minutes

Cook Time: 30 minutes

Servings: 12 squares

Nutrition as per serving:

155kcal / 14g fat / 13g carbs / 10g fiber / 4g protein = 2.8g net carbs

Ingredients

- Avocado, mashed 1 cup

- Vanilla 1/2 tsp

- Cocoa powder 4 tbsp.

- Refined coconut oil (or ghee, butter, lard, shortening) 3 tbsp.

- Eggs 2

- Lily's chocolate chips melted 1/2 cup (100 g)

Dry Ingredients

- Blanched almond flour 3/4 cup

- Baking soda 1/4 tsp

- Baking powder 1 tsp

- Salt 1/4 tsp

- Erythritol 1/4 cup (see sweetener note *1)

- Stevia powder 1 tsp (see sweetener note *1)

Directions

1. Heat the oven up to 350F/ 180C.

2. Sift together the dry ingredients in a small bowl and stir.

3. Place the Peeled avocados in a food processor and process until smooth.

4. One by one, add all the wet ingredients into the food processor, processing every few seconds

5. Now include the dry ingredients into the food processor and blend until combined.

6. Line a parchment paper in a baking dish (of 12"x8") and transfer the batter into it. Spread evenly and put in the heated oven. Cook for 30 minutes or the center springs back to touch. It should be soft to touch.

7. Remove from oven, set aside to cool fully before cutting into 12 slices.

10. Low Carb-1 minute Cinnamon Roll Mug Cake

Prep. Time: 1 minute

Cook Time: 1 minute

Servings: 1 serving

The serving size is 1mug

Nutrition as per serving:

132kcal / 4g fat / 6g carbs / 2g fiber / 25g protein = 4g net carbs

Ingredients

- Protein powder, vanilla flavor 1 scoop
- Baking powder 1/2 tsp
- Coconut flour 1 tbsp.
- Cinnamon 1/2 tsp
- Granulated sweetener 1 tbsp.
- Egg 1 large
- Almond milk, unsweetened 1/4 cup
- Vanilla extract 1/4 tsp
- Granulated sweetener 1 tsp
- Cinnamon 1/2 tsp

For the glaze

- Coconut butter melted 1 tbsp.
- Almond milk 1/2 tsp
- Cinnamon a pinch

Directions

1. Oil a microwave-proof mug. In a small bowl, add the protein powder, coconut flour, baking powder, sweetener, cinnamon and mix well.
2. Add in the egg and stir into the flour mixture. Include the vanilla extract and milk. If the batter is too dry, keep adding milk until a thick consistency is reached.
3. Pour this batter into the oiled mug. Sprinkle extra cinnamon and keto granulated sweetener over the top and swirl. Place in microwave and cook for 60 seconds, or till

the center is just cooked. Do not overcook, or it will come out dry. Drizzle the glaze on top and enjoy!

4. Prepare glaze by mixing all ingredients and use.

11. Double Chocolate Muffins

Prep. Time: 10 minutes

Cook Time: 15 minutes

Servings: 12 muffins

The serving size is 1 muffin

Nutrition as per serving:

280 kcal / 27g fat / 7g carbs / 4g fiber / 7g protein = 3g net carbs

Ingredients

- Almond flour 2 cup
- Cocoa powder unsweetened 3/4 cup
- Swerve sweetener 1/4 cup
- Baking powder 1 1/2 tsp.
- Kosher salt 1 tsp.
- Butter melted 1 cup (2 sticks)
- Eggs 3 large
- Pure vanilla extract 1 tsp.
- Dark chocolate chips, sugar-free (like lily's) 1 cup

Directions

1. Heat oven up to 350° and line cupcake liners in a muffin tin. In a big bowl, stir together almond flour, Swerve, cocoa powder, salt and baking powder. Include eggs, melted butter and vanilla and mix until combined.

2. Stir in the chocolate chips.

3. Pour batter equally in muffin cups and bake for 12 minutes or until the muffin top springs back to touch.

Chapter 4- Keto Fat Bombs

1. Cheesecake Fat Bombs

Prep. Time: 5 minutes

Servings: 24Fat Bombs

The serving size is 1 Fat Bomb

Nutrition as per serving:

108kcal / 12g fat / 1g carbs / 1g fiber / 1g protein = 0g net carbs

Ingredients

- Heavy Cream 4 oz.
- Cream cheese at room temperature 8 oz.
- Erythritol 2-3 tbsp.
- Coconut oil or butter 4 oz.
- Vanilla extracts 2tsp.
- Baking chocolate or coconut for decorating

Directions

1. In a big mixing bowl, add all the ingredients and mix for 1-2 minutes with an electric mixer until well combined and creamy.

2. Spoon mixture into an unlined or lined mini cupcake tin. Chill for 1-2 hours in the refrigerator or freezer for about 30 minutes.

3. Take out from the cupcake tins and store them in a sealed container. It can be refrigerated for up to two weeks.

2. Brownie Fat Bombs

Prep. Time: 15 minutes

Servings: 16 fat bombs

The serving size is 2 fat bombs

Nutrition as per serving:

174 kcal / 16g fat / 4g carbs / 2g fiber / 3g protein = 2g net carbs

Ingredients

- Ghee 1/4 cup

- Cocoa butter 1 oz.

- Vanilla extract 1/2 tsp

- Salt 1/4 tsp

- Raw cacao powder 6 tbsp.

- Swerve Sweetener powdered 1/3 cup

- Water 2 tbsp.

- Almond butter 1/3 cup

- Nuts, chopped (optional) 1/4 cup

Directions

1. melt the cocoa butter and ghee together In a heat-safe bowl placed over a pot of simmering water,

2. Add in the sweetener, cacao powder, salt and vanilla extract. This mixture will be smooth and thin.

3. Stir in the water and beat the mixture till it thickens to the consistency of a thick frosting.

4. Mix in the nut butter with a rubber spatula. The mixture will look like cookie dough. Mix in the coarsely chopped nuts.

5. Shape into 1 inch sized balls (will make about 16) and chill until firm.

3. Coffee Fat Bombs

Prep. Time: 10 minutes

Servings: 8 Fat Bombs

The serving size is 1 Fat Bomb

Nutrition as per serving:

140 kcal / 14g fat / 4g carbs / 2g fiber / 1.5g protein = 2g net carbs

Ingredients

- Cream Cheese, Full-fat 8 Oz.
- Butter Unsalted, ½ cup (1 Stick)
- Instant Coffee 1 to 2 Tbsps.
- Chocolate Chips, Low Carb, heaped ¼ Cup
- Confectioners Erythritol heaped ⅓ Cup
- Cocoa Powder, Unsweetened 1½ Tbsp.

Directions

1. In a large bowl, place the butter and cream cheese (both should be at room temperature)
2. Combine them with an electric mixer until smooth.

3. Then include all the remaining ingredients in the bowl, blending until well-combined

4. Scoop out the batter with a tablespoon or a cookie scoop to make around 12 bombs. Place them on a baking sheet lined with parchment. Chill for about 3 hours.

4. Peanut Butter Fat Bombs

Prep. Time: 10 minutes

Servings: 12 fat bombs

The serving size is 1/2 fat bomb

Nutrition as per serving:

247 kcal / 24.3g fat / 3.2g carbs / 1.2g fiber / 3.6g protein = 2g net carbs

Ingredients

For fat bomb

- Natural peanut butter (no sugar) 3/4 cup

- Coconut oil (melted) 1/2 cup

- Vanilla extract 1 tsp.

- Liquid stevia 3 – 4 drops

- Sea salt 1/4 tsp.

For Ganache

- Coconut oil 6 tbsp.

- Cocoa powder 1 tbsp.

- Liquid stevia 1 – 2 drops

Directions

1. Mix the peanut butter, coconut oil, vanilla extract, salt, and liquid stevia together in a small mixing bowl, beat until creamy and smooth.

2. Line muffin paper cups in a six-cup-muffin tray. Fill each cup with about 3 tbsp. of the peanut butter mixture.

3. Refrigerate for about 1 hour to solidify.

4. Meanwhile, beat together the ingredients for Ganache until it's silky.

5. Drizzle about one tbsp. of the chocolate ganache on every fat bomb.

6. Chill for about 30 minutes and enjoy.

5. Cream Cheese Pumpkin Spiced Fat Bombs

Prep. Time: 10 minutes

Servings: 12 Fat Bombs

The serving size is 1 Fat Bomb

Nutrition as per serving:

80 kcal / 7.5g fat / 2g carbs / 0.25g fiber / 1.5g protein = 1.75g net carbs

Ingredients

- Pure pumpkin ⅔ cup
- Pumpkin pie spice ½ tsp
- Cream cheese, full-fat 8 oz.
- Butter melted 3 tbsps.
- Confectioner's erythritol 3 tbsps.

Directions

1. Place all the ingredients in a large bowl and mix with an electric mixer until combined.

2. Make 12 equal-sized balls from the dough. Place paper liners in a mini-muffin tin and place the PB cookie dough in the muffin tin.

3. Chill for a minimum of 2 hours

Note:

If the pumpkin pie spice is not available, make some with the following ingredients

¼ tsp cinnamon, a pinch of (each) - nutmeg, cloves, ginger and allspice.

6. Brownie Truffles

Prep. Time: 5 minutes

Cook Time: 5 minutes

Servings: 20 Truffles

The serving size is 1 Truffle

Nutrition as per serving:

97kcal / 8g fat / 5g carbs / 3g fiber / 4g protein = 2g net carbs

Ingredients

- Sticky sweetener, keto-friendly 1/2 cup of choice
- Homemade Nutella 2 cups
- Coconut flour 3/4 cup (or almond flour 1 ½ cup)
- Chocolate chips, sugar-free 2 cups

Directions

1. Combine the coconut/almond flour, sticky sweetener and chocolate spread in a big mixing bowl. Add a bit more syrup or liquid; if the mixture is too thick, it should become a creamy dough.
2. Place parchment paper on a large plate. Shape into small balls with your hands, and set on the plate. Chill.
3. Melt the sugar-free chocolate chips. Take the truffles from the refrigerator. Immediately, coat each truffle with the melted chocolate, making sure all are evenly coated.
4. Set back on the lined
5. Plate and chill until firm.

7. Coconut Strawberry Fat Bombs

Prep. Time: 10 minutes

Servings: 20 fat bombs

The serving size is 1fat Bomb

Nutrition as per serving:

132kcals / 14.3g fat / 0.9g carbs / 0g fiber / 0.4g protein = 0.9g net carbs

Ingredients

For Coconut base:

- Coconut cream 1 1/2 cups
- Coconut oil (melted) 1/2 cup
- Stevia liquid 1/2 tsp.
- Lime juice 1 tbsp.

For Strawberry topping:

- Fresh chopped strawberries 2 oz.
- Coconut oil (melted) 1/2 cup
- Liquid stevia 5 – 8 drops

Directions

Prepare the coconut base:

1. In a high-speed blender, place all the coconut base ingredients and blend them completely until combined and smooth.
2. Distribute the mixture evenly into an ice cube tray, muffin tray, or a candy mold, leaving room for the topping.
3. Chill in the freezer to set for about 20 minutes.

For the Strawberry topping:

1. In a blender, put all the ingredients for the strawberry topping, then blend until smooth.

2. When the base is set, spoon the strawberry mixture equally over each one.

3. Refrigerate the fat bombs for about 2 hours and enjoy.

8. Raspberry & White Chocolate Fat Bombs

Prep. Time: 5 minutes

Servings: 10-12 fat bombs

The serving size is 1 fat Bomb

Nutrition as per serving:

153kcal / 16g fat / 1.5g carbs / 0.4g fiber / 0.2g protein = 1.2g net carbs

Ingredients

- Cacao butter 2 oz.
- Coconut oil 1/2 cup
- Raspberries freeze-dried 1/2 cup
- Erythritol sweetener, powdered (like swerve) 1/4 cup

Directions

1. Place paper liners in a 12-cup muffin pan.
2. In a small pot, heat the cacao butter and coconut oil on low flame until melted completely. Take off the pot from heat.
3. Blend the freeze-dried raspberries in a blender or food processor, or coffee grinder.
4. Include the sweetener and powdered berries into the pot, stirring to dissolve the sweetener.

5. Distribute the mixture evenly between the muffin cups. Don't worry if the raspberry powder sinks to the bottom. Just stir the mixture when pouring them into each mold to distribute the raspberry powder in each mold.

6. Chill until hard. Enjoy.

9. Almond Joy Fat Bombs (3 Ingredients)

Prep. Time: 2 minutes

Cook Time: 3 minutes

Servings: 24 cups

The serving size is 1 cup

Nutrition as per serving:

72kcal / 8g fat / 6g carbs / 4g fiber / 2g protein = 2g net carbs

Ingredients

- Coconut butter softened 1/4 cup
- Chocolate chips, sugar-free, divided 20 oz.
- Almonds 24 whole

Directions

1. Place muffin liners in a 24-cup mini muffin tin and put them aside.

2. Melt 3/4 of the sugar-free chocolate chips in a microwave-proof bowl. Distribute the chocolate mixture equally into all the muffin liners. Also, scrape down all the chocolate coated on the sides. Chill until firm.

3. When the chocolate is hard, spoon in the melted coconut butter evenly into every chocolate cup, leaving room for chocolate filling on top. Add in more softened coconut butter if needed.

4. Melt the rest of the chocolate chips and with it, cover each of the chocolate coconut cups. Place an almond on top of each cup and chill until firm.

10. Pecan pie fat bombs

Prep. Time: 15 minutes

Servings: 18 balls

The serving size is 2 balls

Nutrition as per serving

121 kcal / 12g fat / 3.8g carbs / 2.9g fiber / 2g protein = 0.9g net carbs

Ingredients

- Pecans, (or any nut) 1½ cup s
- Coconut butter, ¼ cup
- Coconut shredded ½ cup
- Chia seeds 2 tbsp.
- Pecan butter (or any nut butter) 2 tbsp.
- Flax meal 2 tbsp.
- Coconut oil 1tsp.
- Hemp seeds 2 tbsp.
- Vanilla extract ½tsp.
- Cinnamon 1½tsp.
- Kosher salt ¼tsp.

Directions

1. Add the ingredients altogether in a food processor. Process for a minute or two to break down the mixture. First, it will become powdery. Then it will stick together but remain crumbly.

2. Continue to process until the oils begin to expel a bit, and the mixture will begin to stick together easily –be cautious not to process excessively, or you will have nut butter.

3. Using a tablespoon or small cookie scooper, scoop to make equal pieces of the mixture. Roll them into balls with your hands placing them all on a large plate. Chill for about 30 mins.

4. Keep in a sealed container or a zip-lock bag in the freezer or refrigerator.

11. PB. Cookie Dough Fat Bomb

Prep. Time: 10 minutes

Servings: 12 Fat Bombs

The serving size is 1 Fat Bomb

Nutrition as per serving:

135kcal / 11g fat / 5g carbs / 3.5g fiber / 4g protein = 1.5g net carbs

Ingredients

- Lily's chocolate chips ⅓ cup
- Almond flour, superfine 1 cup
- Natural peanut butter 6 tbsps.
- Confectioner's erythritol 2 tbsps.
- Coconut oil (melted) 1 tbsps.
- Vanilla extract 1 tsp
- Salt, a pinch

Directions

1. Place all the ingredients in a large bowl and mix with a spoon until crumbly.

2. Form a dough ball with your hands.

3. Line parchment paper on a baking sheet. Scoop out equal-sized 12 cookie dough fat bombs.

4. Chill for about an hour

5. Once they are done setting, keep in a sealed bag in the fridge.

Conclusion

When going on a ketogenic diet, one retains modest protein consumption but increases their fat intake. The transition to a low-carb diet brings your body into a ketosis state, where fat is used for energy compared to carbohydrates.

It takes some time for fats to decompose through the digestive tract and delay the decomposition of the carbohydrates into sugar, maintain our blood sugar concentrations steady and allow us to feel satiated longer. Based on observational evidence, incorporating a tablespoonful of coconut oil into your diet every day may also result in lower weight.

You may also need to monitor the portion sizes, but as fat is intrinsically pleasing, having one for breakfast will help deter eating during meals.

When consuming high-fat meals, including keto fat bombs, you will further encourage weight reduction by decreasing appetite for the next meal. Be it fat bombs or cheesy waffles or any other hi fat low-carb dessert, they are a dieter's dream come true.

Following the keto diet can positively impact one's brain function.

Advantages of the ketogenic diet and fat bombs.

Keto fat bombs may be seen as a way to reduce sugar habits.

Ketogenic fat bombs are simple to produce, easy to keep, and easy to eat; they often need fewer ingredients than other foods.

Ketogenic fat bombs are tasty and have a broad variety of low-carb recipes.

Ketogenic fat bombs are quick to produce, are easy to store, and are ready to consume at any time.

In this book, you will find the best and easy to prepare keto cakes, chaffles, and yummy high-fat recipes that will fulfill your cravings for desserts after meals or snacks when you don't feel too hungry. Enjoy these recipes by yourself, or even better, share the joy with family and friends!

The Complete Ketogenic Guidebook for Women Over 50

By

Keto Flex Academy

Table of contents

Introduction

A Keto diet is one that is very low in carbohydrates but rich in fats and is normal on protein. Through the years, the Keto diet has been used to treat a variety of diseases that people have learned to face. This includes: rectifying weight gain as well as managing or treating diseases of human beings like treating epilepsy in youngsters. The Keto diet enables the human body to use its fats instead of consuming its carbohydrates. Typically, the body's carbohydrates, which are present in the foods you eat, are transformed into glucose. Glucose is a consequence of the body burning off its carbohydrates which are typically distributed throughout the body. A dietary strategy and a balanced lifestyle are, thus, an important necessity for all the citizens who choose to prevent early mortality. Health problems are widely prevalent in women over the age of 50 since they suffer from normal bodily adjustments related to menopause.

Osteoporosis, hypertension, high blood pressure, overweight, and inflammation are popular among women of this category. An effective metabolism is a secret to good health! The level of metabolism does not stay the same, though! As an individual age, the body naturally moves through a slow metabolic phase. This phase of aging speeds up as we eat unhealthy food and live an unhealthy lifestyle, resulting in a variety of metabolic disorders and other associated diseases. It's a popular myth that you'll be consuming bland and fatty food while you're on a ketogenic diet. Although basic foods are a necessity, there are so many ways to bring the spice back into your diet.

Doing keto doesn't just include consuming any type of fat or having ice cream on the mouth. Instead, it's about choosing products that are high in healthy fats and poor in carbohydrates cautiously. If you aren't sure where to go, don't be afraid. Some really good, fantastic keto meals are out there promising to be eaten.

Chapter 1: Introduction to Ketogenic Diet

A ketogenic diet is widely known as a diet which is low in carbs and in which the human body generates ketones to be processed as energy in the liver. Several different names are related to a keto diet, lower-carb diet, lower-carb high fat (LCHF), etc. Patterns of diet come and go, and it seems like the formula mostly includes a low-carb plan. At the top of the chart right now is the ketogenic diet. The keto diet, also referred to as the ketogenic diet, relies on having more of the calories from protein and a few from fat while eliminating carbohydrates dramatically.

1.1 How Does The Ketogenic Diet Work?

A high fat, medium protein, low carbohydrate diet plan, which varies from standard, balanced eating recommendations, is the ketogenic diet. Many foods abundant in nutrients, including vegetables, fruits, whole grains, milk products, are sources of carbohydrates. Carbs from both types are highly constrained on a keto diet. Keto dieters, therefore, do not eat bread, grains, or cereals with the intention of holding carbs below 50 g a day. And since them, too, contain carbohydrates, even fruits and vegetables are restricted. The keto diet involves making drastic changes about how they normally consume for most individuals.

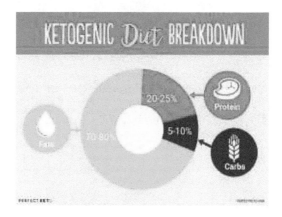

What is Ketosis?

Ketosis is a metabolic condition where the body utilizes fat and ketones as the main source of fuel instead of glucose (sugar).

A critical part of beginning a keto diet is knowing how Ketosis works. Ketosis, irrespective of the number of carbohydrates you consume, is a phase that the body goes through on a daily basis. This is because if sugar is not readily accessible, this method provides humans energy from ketones.

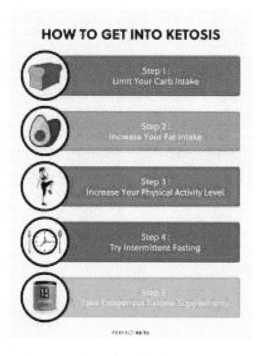

The body tends to raise its ketone levels if the requirement for energy grows, and carbohydrates are not sufficient to satisfy the need. If a more extended period of time (i.e., more than three days) is limited to carbohydrates, the body can raise ketone levels much more. These deeper ketosis rates produce several favorable benefits in the body, results that are achieved when adopting the ketogenic diet is the best and healthiest manner practicable.

Most individuals, however, seldom get Ketosis and never feel its advantages because the body tends to use sugar as its main source of power, even if the diet provides plenty of carbohydrates and protein.

How does Ketosis happen?

The body would turn any of its accumulated fat into extremely effective energy molecules called ketones while the body has no access to healthy food, like while you are resting, exercising, or adopting a ketogenic diet. (We should credit our body's capacity to alter metabolic processes for that.) After the body breaks down fat into glycerol and fatty acids, such ketones are synthesized.

While in certain cells in the body, fatty acids and glycerol may be directly converted into food, brain cells do not use them as energy at all. This really is because they are so gradually processed into energy to help the brain work.

That's why sugar appears to be the brain's primary source of fuel. Interestingly, this also enables one to realize that we make ketones. Thus providing an alternate source of energy, because we do not eat sufficient calories, our brain will be incredibly susceptible. Our muscles will be quickly broken down and transformed into glucose to support our brains that are sugar-hungry before we have enough power left to find food. The human species would most definitely be endangered without ketones.

1.2 Types of Ketogenic Diet

There are a variety of aspects in which ketosis can be induced, and so there are a number of diverse ketogenic diet variations.

Keto Diet Standard (SKD)

This is a really low carb diet, a medium protein diet yet high fat. Usually, it comprises 70 to 75% fat, 20% protein, and only 5 to 10% carbohydrates.

A traditional standard ketogenic diet, in terms of grams per day, will be:

- Carbohydrate between 20-50g

- Around 40-60g of protein

- No limit specified for fat

The bulk of calories should be given by fat in the diet for this to be a keto diet. As energy needs might differ greatly among individuals, no limit is set. A large number of vegetables, especially non-starchy veggies, should be included in ketogenic diets, as they are very low in carbs.

In order to help people reduce weight, increase blood glucose regulation and improve cardiac health, standardized ketogenic diets have repeatedly demonstrated success.

Very-low-carb diet ketogenic (VLCKD)

Very-low-carb is a traditional ketogenic diet, and so a VLCKD would normally correspond to a traditional ketogenic diet.

Ketogenic Diet Well Formulated (WFKD)

The word 'Well Formulated Keto Diet' derives from one of the main ketogenic diet experts, Steve Phinney.

As a traditional ketogenic diet, the WFKD maintains a similar blueprint. Well-developed ensures that weight, protein & carbohydrate macronutrients align with the ratios of the traditional ketogenic diet and thus have the greatest likelihood of ketosis happening.

Ketogenic Diet MCT

This fits the description of the traditional ketogenic diet but insists on providing more of the diet's fat content through the use of medium-chain triglycerides (MCTs). MCTs are present in coconut oil and are accessible in the liquid state of MCT oil and MCT dispersant.

To treat epilepsy, MCT ketogenic diets are being used since the idea is that MCTs enable individuals to absorb more carbohydrates and protein, thus sustaining ketosis. That's because multiple ketones per gram of fat are produced by MCTs than the long-chain triglycerides found in natural dietary fat. There is a dearth of research, though, exploring whether MCTs have greater advantages on weight loss and blood sugar.

Ketogenic diet Calorie-restricted

Unless calories are reduced to a fixed number, a calorie-restricted ketogenic diet is identical to a normal ketogenic diet.

Research indicates that, whether calorie consumption is reduced or not, ketogenic diets seem to be effective. This is because it helps to avoid over-eating of itself from the nutritious impact of eating fat and staying in ketosis.

The Ketogenic Cyclical Diet (CKD)

There are days on which more carbohydrates are ingested, like five ketogenic days accompanied by two high carbohydrate days, in the CKD diet, frequently recognized as carb back loading.

The diet is meant for athletes who can regenerate glycogen drained from muscles during exercises using the high carbohydrate days.

Ketogenic Diet Targeted (TKD)

Even though carbs are eaten around exercise hours, the TKD is equivalent to a typical ketogenic diet. It is a combination between a regular ketogenic diet as well as a cyclical ketogenic diet that requires every day you work out to eat carbohydrates.

It is focused on the assumption that carbohydrates eaten before or during a physical effort can be absorbed even more effectively, while the need for energy from the muscles rises while we are engaged.

Ketogenic Diet of High Protein

With a proportion of 35 percent protein, 60 percent fat, and 5 percent carbohydrates, this diet contains more protein than a regular keto diet.

For people who need to lose weight, a study shows that a high-protein keto is beneficial for weight loss. Like in other types of the ketogenic diet, if practiced for several years, there is an absence of research on which there are any health risks.

1.3 Benefits of Ketogenic Diet

A keto diet has many advantages, including:

Weight Reduction

A person's keto diet will help them lose weight. The keto diet help encourages weight loss in many aspects, particularly metabolism boosting and appetite reduction. Ketogenic diets comprise foods that load up an individual and can minimize hormones that trigger appetite. For these factors, it may suppress appetite and encourage weight loss by adopting a keto diet.

Helps improve acne

In certain persons, acne has many common reasons and can have associations with diet and blood sugar. Consuming a diet rich in highly processed carbs can change the equivalence of intestinal bacteria and cause major rises and declines in blood sugar, both of which would negatively impact the health of the skin.

It can decrease the risk of certain cancers.

The implications of the ketogenic diet have been studied by experts to potentially avoid or even cure some cancers. One research showed that in patients with some cancers, a ketogenic diet could be a healthy and appropriate complementary medication to be used in addition to chemotherapy and radiation therapy. This is because, in cancer cells, it might cause greater oxidative stress than in regular cells, allowing them to die.

It can safeguard brain function.

Some research indicates that neuroprotective advantages are offered by the ketones developed during the ketogenic diet that indicates they can reinforce and defend the brain and nerve cells.

A ketogenic diet might help a person resist or maintain problems such as Alzheimer's disease for this purpose.

Lessens seizures potentially

In a ketogenic diet, the proportion of fat, protein, and carbohydrates changes the way the body utilizes energy, results in ketosis. Ketosis is a biochemical mechanism in which ketone bodies are being used by the body for energy.

The Epilepsy Foundation indicates that ketosis in people with epilepsy, particularly those who have not adapted to other types of treatment, might decrease seizures. More study is required on how efficient this is, as it seems to have the greatest influence on children who have generalized seizures.

Improves the effects of PCOS

Polycystic ovary syndrome (PCOS) may contribute to surplus male hormones, ovulatory instability, and polycystic ovaries as a hormonal syndrome. In individuals with PCOS, a high-carbohydrate diet can trigger negative impacts, like skin problems as well as excess weight.

The researchers observed that many markers of PCOS are strengthened by a ketogenic diet, including:

- Loss in weight

- Balance of hormones

- Ratios of follicle-stimulating hormone (LH) and luteinizing hormone (LH) (FSH)

- Insulin fasting levels

A different research analysis showed that for people with hormonal conditions, like PCOS and type 2 diabetes, a keto diet has positive benefits. They also cautioned, though, that the findings were too diverse to prescribe a keto diet as a specific PCOS treatment.

Chapter 2: Easy ketogenic Low Carb Recipes

It may be challenging to adopt different diets: all the foods to quit, to consume more, to purchase new products. It's enough to make bonkers for everyone. But the ketogenic, or "keto," diet, as well as its keto meals, are one type of eating that has been gathering traction lately.

Doing keto doesn't only involve eating some sort of fat or putting ice cream on your mouth. Rather, it's about picking items that are rich in good fats and low in carbohydrates carefully. If you aren't sure where to start, don't be scared. Some very healthy, excellent keto meals are out there appealing to be consumed.

2.1 Keto Breakfast Recipes

1. HIGH PROTEIN COTTAGE CHEESE OMELET

Serving: 1

Preparation time: 5 minutes

Nutritional Values: 250kcal Calories | 18g Fat | 4 g Carbs | 18.7g Proteins

Ingredients

- 2 eggs - large

- 1 tbsp. of whole milk or 2% milk

- Kosher salt about 1/8 tsp.

- Pinch of black pepper, freshly ground,

- 1/2 tbsp. of butter - unsalted

- 1 cup spinach (about 1 ounce)

- Cottage cheese 3 tbsp.

Directions

1. In a moderate pan, put the eggs, milk, salt, & pepper and stir until the whites & yolks are thoroughly combined, and the eggs are a little viscous.

2. In an 8-inch non - stick roasting pan over medium heat, add the butter. Flip the pan until the butter covers the bottom equally. Include the spinach and simmer for around 30 seconds before it is ripened. Put the eggs in and turn the pan directly so that the eggs cover the whole bottom.

3. To softly pull and move the cooked eggs from the sides into the middle of the pan, use either a silicone or rubber spatula, leaving room for the raw eggs and creating waves in the omelet. Rig a spatula underneath the edges to enable raw eggs to run beneath the cooked part, holding and swiveling the pan. Cook for around 2 minutes until the sides are settled, and the middle is moist but no longer soft or gooey.

4. Let the pan away from the heat. Whisk over half the eggs with the cottage cheese. Cover the egg carefully over the filling using a spatula. On a plate, transfer the omelet.

2. DEVILED EGGS

Serving: 4-6

Preparation time: 15-20 minutes

Nutritional values: 280kcal Calories | 23g Fat | 3.4g Carbs | 15g Proteins

Ingredients

- 12 eggs - large
- 8 oz. of full-fat cream cheese, warmed for 1 hour or more at room temperature,
- Kosher salt about 1/2 teaspoon
- 1 shred of black pepper
- 2 tablespoons of all the bagel seasoning

Directions

1. A dozen eggs become hardboiled according to your chosen method. (The most critical part is to layer with ice water, raise to a boil, then lift from the heat and leave for 8 to 10 minutes to remain.) In an ice bucket, soak and chill the eggs. And peel them.

2. Cut the eggs laterally in half and use a tiny spoon to pick the yolks out and put them in a dish.

3. Take the cream cheese and transfer it to the yolks into rough parts. Use a hand beater or stick mixer to mix until smooth and blended, starting at lower speeds and then at high speed. Bang in the pepper and salt. Uh, taste. If needed, tweak the seasonings.

4. Load the egg whites with the yolk mixture using a spoon or piping bag. (It would be stiff; to soften it any further if possible, microwave it in very fast bursts of 2 to 3 seconds.)

5. With the all-bagel seasoning, dust the tops of the loaded eggs appropriately. In two hours, serve.

3. 90 SECOND KETO BREAD

Serving: 1

Preparation time: 90 seconds

Nutritional values: 99kcal Calories | 8.5g Fat | 2g Carbs | 3.9g Proteins

Instructions

- 1 egg - large

- 1 spoonful of milk

- Olive oil about 1 tablespoon

- 1 tablespoon flour of coconut

- 1 tablespoon flour of almonds or hazelnuts

- 1/4 tsp. powder for baking

- Pinch of salt

Add-ins optional:

- 1/4 cup of grated cheese

- 1 tbsp. scallions or herbs chopped

Directions

1. In a small cup, mix together the egg, milk, oil, coconut flour, almond flour, baking powder, and salt. If using, incorporate cheese and scallions or herbs and mix to blend.

2. To induce any air bubbles to lift and burst, pour into a wide microwave-safe mug and strike the bottom tightly on the counter multiple times. Reheat for 1 minute, 30 seconds, on maximum.

3. On a chopping board, transpose the mug and enable the bread to drop out. Slice into 1/2-inch-thick strips crosswise. For the toast, heat a teaspoon of oil across moderate flame in a small pan until it glistens. Add the strips and toast, around 30 seconds on either side, before golden-brown.

4. KETO FRITTATA

Serving: 4-6

Preparation time: 25 minutes

Nutritional values: 155kcal Calories | 8.9g Fat | 11.4g Carbs | 7.9g Proteins

Instructions

- 6 large eggs, sufficient for the ingredients to fill

- Heavy cream 1/4 cup

- 1 tsp. of kosher salt, split-up

- 4 thick-cut bacon (8 oz.) pieces, diced (optional)

- 2 tiny, stripped, and finely diced Yukon gold potatoes

- 1/4 tsp. of black pepper, freshly ground

- 2 cups of spinach (2 ounces)

- Garlic 2 cloves, chopped.

- 2 tsp. of fresh leaves of thyme

- 1 cup of Gruyere, Fontina, or Cheddar crushed cheese

Directions

1. Preheat oven. In the center of the oven, position a brace and warm it to 400 °F.

2. Stir together the cream and eggs. In a medium bowl, stir together the eggs, whipping cream, and 1/2 teaspoon salt; hold.

3. Just prepare the bacon. Put the bacon in a non - stick 10-12-inch cold cooking pan or cast-iron skillet, and keep the heat to moderate. Cook the bacon until translucent, stirring regularly, for 8 to 10 minutes. Move the bacon to a paper towel-lined dish with a slotted spoon and skim off all but 2 tbsp. of the fat. (If the bacon is excluded, heat the pan with 2 tablespoons of oil, then finish incorporating the potatoes).

4. Simmer the potatoes in the fat of the bacon. Mix the potatoes and spray with the pepper and the remaining 1/2 teaspoon salt. Switch the pan to a moderate flame. Heat, stirring regularly, for 4 to 6 minutes, until soft and golden brown.

5. Crumble the spinach with thyme & garlic. Put the spinach, garlic, and thyme in the pan and cook, mixing, for 30 seconds to 1 minute, or until the spinach is wilted. Transfer the bacon again to the skillet and swirl to spread uniformly.

6. Add some cheese. Scattered the vegetables, compressed with a spatula, into an even layer. Over the top, spread the cheese and let it only begin to melt.

7. In the pan, add the egg mixture. Place over the vegetables and cheese with the egg mixture. To be sure that the eggs settle equally over all the vegetables, rotate the skillet. Wait for a minute or two before you observe the eggs starting to set at the ends of the pan.

8. Around 8 to 10 minutes, oven the frittata. Bake for 8 to 10 minutes unless the eggs are ready. Cut a tiny slit in the middle of the frittata to test. Bake for a few more minutes if uncooked eggs run into the cut; if the eggs are fixed, take the frittata out

of the oven. At the end of cooking, hold the frittata underneath the broiler for a couple of minutes for a crisped, charred layer.

9. For 5 minutes, chill in the skillet, then cut into slices and serve.

5. CHEESE, HAM, AND EGG WRAPS

Serving: 4

Preparation time: 15-20 minutes

Nutritional values: 371kcal calories | 27g Fat | %g Carbs | 27g Proteins

Ingredients

- 8 eggs - large

- 4 tsp. of Water

- 2 tsp. of all-purpose or cornstarch flour

- Half a teaspoon of fine salt

- 4 tsp. of coconut or vegetable oil

- 1 1/3 cups of Swiss grated cheese

- 4 ounces of ham extremely thinly sliced

- 1 1/3 cups of watercress loosely wrapped

Directions

1. In a wide bowl, put the eggs, water, flour or cornflour, and salt, and stir until the starch or cornflour is fully dissolved.

2. In a 12-inch non - stick saucepan, heat 1 tsp. Of oil unless glinting, over moderate flame. To cover the surface with the oil, move the pan. To brush the bottom part in a thin coating, incorporate 1/2 cup of the egg mixture and stir. Cook for 3 to 6 minutes before the wrapping is fully set on the sides and on the surface (the top may be a little damp but should be apparently set).

3. Soften the sides of the wrap using a wide spatula and move it under the wrap, ensuring that it will slide across the pan quickly. With the spatula, turn the wrap. Slather 1/3 cup of cheese instantly over the wrap and simmer for around 1 minute before the second side is ready. Drop it onto a chopping board or work surface (the cheese may not be completely melted yet). Put a single coat of ham over the egg when it is still hot. Put 1/3 of a cup of watercress in the middle of the wrap. Firmly roll it up.

4. Repeat the leftover wraps by cooking and filling them. Slice each wrap crosswise into 6 (1-inch) bits using a steak knife.

6. BACON GRUYERE EGG BITES

Serving: 9

Preparation time: 10-20 minutes

Nutritional values: 208kcal Calories | 18g Fat | 1g Carbs | 11g Proteins

Ingredients

- Fat or butter of bacon, to coat the pan

- 9 large eggs

- 3/4 cup Gruyere cheese grated (2 1/4 oz.)

- 1/3 cup (about 2 1/2 oz.) cream cheese

- Kosher salt about 1/2 teaspoon

- 6 pieces of thick-cut, cooked, and imploded bacon

Directions

1. In the center of the oven, place a rack and warm it to 350°F. Graciously cover an 8x8-inch (broiler-safe if you like a crisped top) cooking dish with bacon fat or butter.

2. Put the eggs, Gruyere, cream cheese, and salt in a mixer and combine for around 1 minute, at moderate speed, until quite smooth. Drop it into the pan for baking. Slather bacon with it. With aluminum foil, cover firmly.

3. Take the oven rack out from the oven midway. Upon on the oven rack, put a roasting tray. Put in 6 extremely hot tap water pots. Place the baking dish in the hot skillet with the eggs. Bake until the center is just ready, 55 minutes to 1 hour.

4. Pull the roasting pan from the oven cautiously. Remove the roasting pan from the baking dish and unfold it. (For a browned surface: Heat the oven to sauté. Sauté 4 to 5 minutes before the top is golden-brown.) Slice and serve into 9 squares.

7. RADISH TURNIP AND FRIED EGGS HASH WITH GREEN GARLIC

Serving: 2

Preparation time: 10-12 minutes

Nutritional values: 392kcal calories | 34g Fat | 10g Carbs | 13g Proteins

Ingredients

- 2 to 3 tiny turnips (approximately 1 1/2 cups cubed) clipped, peeled, and sliced into 3/4-inch cubes

- 4 to 5 tiny, rinsed and clipped radishes, and sliced into 3/4-inch cubes (approximately 1 1/2 cubed cups)

- Crushed Salt of the Sea

- Pepper freshly crushed

- 2 tbsp. of grapeseed oil, or other heat-tolerant, neutral oil

- 1 green garlic stalk, clipped and diced (just white and light green parts)

- 2 spoonful's of unsalted butter

- Four eggs

- 1 tablespoon parsley chopped

Directions

1. Place the water in a wide skillet and raise it to a boil. Stir in 2 teaspoons of sea salt. Transfer to a bowl with a slotted spoon, skim off any extra water and set it aside. Simmer turnip cubes only until moist, 3 to 4 minutes. Next, quickly boil the

radishes for 30 to 60 seconds; scrape with a slotted spoon in a pan, skim off any extra water, and set it aside.

2. Place a sauté pan of cast iron over moderate flame. Include the grapeseed oil and add the turnips & radishes when warm, and pinch the sea salt and pepper with each one. Cook for 8 minutes or until golden-brown, flipping vegetables just once or twice. Switch the heat to medium, bring in the green garlic and simmer for a minute or so. Place the vegetables to the edges, melt the butter in the center of the pan, and add the eggs. Cook unearthed for 4 to 6 minutes for over-easy eggs; close pan for 3 minutes for over-medium eggs, then unfold and continue to cook only until whites are ready, 2 to 3 minutes further. To taste, finish with chopped parsley and sea salt and pepper. Instantly serve.

8. CAULIFLOWER RICE BURRITO BOWLS

Serving: 4

Preparation time: 20-25 minutes

Nutritional values: 374kcal Calories | 15g Fat | 46g Carbs | 21g Protein

Ingredients

- 1 (15-ounce) canned washed and cleaned black beans.

- 1 cup of corn kernels - frozen

- 2 spoonful's of water

- Chili powder about 1/2 teaspoon

- 1/2 teaspoon of cumin powder

- 3/4 teaspoon of kosher salt, distributed

- 1 tablespoon of olive oil

- One cauliflower of a medium head (just around 1 1/2 lbs.), riced (or one 16oz sack riced cauliflower)

- 1/3 cup of fresh cilantro minced, distributed

- 1/4 cup of lime juice, freshly extracted (from 2 to 3 lemons)

- 1 cup roasted chicken chopped or shredded (optional), warmed if necessary

- 1 cup of gallo pico de or salsa

- One large, drained, pitted, and diced avocado

Directions

1. In a small pan, put the beans, corn, water, chili powder, cumin, and 1/4 tsp. over moderate flame. Cook for 3 to 5 minutes, mixing periodically until hot. Distance yourself from the steam.

2. In the meantime, over a moderate flame, heat the oil in a wide, large skillet until it shimmers. Transfer the cauliflower and the residual 1/2 teaspoon salt to the mixture. Process until the cauliflower is cooked through though soft, 3 to 5 minutes, mixing periodically. Remove from the heat. Transfer the cilantro and lime juice to 1/4 cup and mix to blend.

3. Divide into four bowls the riced cauliflower. Cover with the mixture of bean and corn, chicken if used, pico de gallo or salsa, and pieces of avocado. Slather with the cilantro that persists and serve hot.

9. KETO LOAF

Serving: 1

Preparation time: 10-12 minutes

Nutritional values: 239kcal Calories | 22g Fat | 4g carbs | 8g Proteins

Ingredients

- Two cups of fine powdered almond flour, especially brands like King Arthur

- 1 tsp. powder for baking

- 1/2 tsp. of gum xanthan

- Kosher salt about 1\2 tsp.

- 7 eggs - large

- 8 tbsp. (1 stick) of melted and chilled unsalted butter

- 2 tbsp. of concentrated, processed, and chilled coconut oil

Directions

1. In the center of the oven, place a rack and warm it to 351°F. Cover the bottom part of a parchment paper 9x5-inch metallic loaf pan, having the surplus spill around the long sides to create a loop. Just set aside.

2. In a wide dish, mix together the flour of almond, powder for baking, xanthan gum, as well as salt. Just placed back.

3. Put the eggs in a bowl equipped with the whisk extension of a stand blender. Beat at moderate pressure until soft and drippy. Lower the level to moderate, incorporate the butter and oil of coconut gradually, and whisk unless well mixed. Lessen the intensity to medium, incorporate the mixture of almond flour

gradually, and mix unless mixed. Rise the pace to moderate and beat for around 1 minute before the mixture thickens.

4. Pour and scrape the top into the primed pan. Bake for 45 to 55 minutes unless a knife placed in the middle comes out clean. Let it cool for around ten minutes in the pan. Take the loaf over the skillet, grab the parchment paper, and shift it to a cutting board. Cool it down completely until slicing.

10. BREAKFAST SALAD

Serving: 4

Preparation time: 10 minutes

Nutritional values: 425kcal Calories | 34g Fat | 16g Carbs | 17g Proteins

Ingredients

- Spinach 8 Oz (about 6 packed cups)

- 1/2 a cup of blueberries

- 1 medium-sized avocado, chopped

- 1/3 cup red roasted quinoa

- 1/4 cup of pumpkin seeds - toasted

- Bacon - 6 strips

- 4 eggs of large size

- 1/4 cup of apple cider vinegar

- 2 tsp. of honey

- Kosher salt about 1\2 tsp.

Directions

1. In a large bowl, add the spinach, avocado, berries, pumpkin seeds, and quinoa and toss them to mix. Distribute the salad into deep plates or pots.

2. Put the bacon over moderate heat in a large cast-iron pan. Cook until the fat has dried out and the bacon is crunchy, tossing halfway around for a total of around 10 minutes. Shift the bacon to a tray that is lined with paper towels. Cut the bacon into little crumbles until it is cold.

3. Lower the heat and fry the eggs to the perfect braising in the dried bacon fat. Keep the pan away from the heat. Place the toppled bacon and an egg on top of each salad.

4. Upon emulsification, mix the vinegar, honey, and salt into the residual bacon fat in the dish. Sprinkle over the salad with the warm dressing and serve promptly.

2.2 Keto Lunch & Dinner Recipes

1. CAULIFLOWER FRIED RICE

Serving: 4

Preparation time: 20- 25 minutes

Nutritional values: 108kcal Calories | 1g Fat | 21g Carbs | 7g Proteins

Ingredients

For Fried Rice

- 1 cauliflower head, sliced into cloves

- Balanced Oil 2 tbsp. (such as vegetable, coconut, or peanut)

- 1 bunch of finely sliced scallions

- 3 cloves of garlic, chopped

- 1 tbsp. natural ginger diced

- 2 peeled and finely chopped carrots

- 2 stalks of celery, chopped

- 1 bell pepper, red, chopped

- 1 cup of peas - frozen

- 2 tbsp. vinegar for rice

- 3 spoonful's of soy sauce

- Sriracha 2 tsp., or enough to taste

For Garnishing

- Balanced oil about 1tbsp. (such as vegetable, coconut, or peanut)

- Four eggs

- Salt and black pepper finely processed

- 4 tbsp. of fresh cilantro, diced

- 4 tbsp. of scallions thinly diced

- 4 tsp. of seeds of sesame

Directions

1. **For Fried Rice:** Pump the cauliflower in the mixing bowl for 2 or 3 minutes before the mishmash resembles rice. Just set aside.

2. Heat oil over a moderate flame in a wide skillet. Include the scallions, garlic, and ginger and mix for around 1 minute, unless aromatic.

3. Incorporate the carrots, celery & red bell pepper, and braise for 9 to 11 minutes until the veggies are soft.

4. Add the cauliflower rice, then stir-fry for another 3 to 5 minutes, once it starts to turn golden. To blend, mix in the frozen peas and toss properly.

5. To combine, incorporate rice vinegar, Sriracha, and soy sauce & swirl. Just set aside.

6. **For Garnishing:** Add the oil in a large skillet over moderate to high flame. Crack the eggs straight into the skillet and stir for 3 to 4 minutes before the whites are assertive, but the yolks are still watery. With pepper and salt, sprinkle each one.

7. Distribute the cauliflower rice into four dishes to serving and serve each one with a fried egg. Sprinkle with 1 tablespoon of cilantro, 1 tablespoon of scallions, and 1 teaspoon of sesame seeds on each dish. Instantly serve then.

2. LOW CARB THAI CURRY SOUP

Serving: 6

Preparation time: 22 minutes

Nutritional values: 324kcal Calories | 27g Fat | 7g Carbs | 15g Proteins

Ingredients

- 4 Leg pieces of boneless skinless chicken,

- 14.5 ounces (411.07 g) full-fat coconut milk

- 2 tsp. of Thai paste of yellow curry

- 2 tsp. of fish sauce

- Three tsp. of Soy Sauce

- 1 tsp. of Agave or honey nectar

- 2 green Scallions minced

- Garlic 4 cloves, minced

- 2 inch (2 inches) coarsely chopped diced ginger

Veggies to add in soup

- One Can of Straw Mushrooms (optional)

- 74.5 g (1/2 cup) of Cherry Tomatoes, half-sliced

- Cilantro, 1/4 cup (4 g), diced

- 3 green Scallions diced

- 1 lime, juiced

Directions

For the Instant Pot

1. Put the essential soup components and lock in an Instant Pot.

2. Process it under heat for 12 minutes by using the SOUP key. The soup button avoids it from boiling and extracting the coconut milk.

3. Discharge the pressure immediately and detach and cut the chicken. Place it in the broth again.

4. Transfer the warm broth to the vegetables. In the hot broth, you want to bring them a little scorching but not to mold them though you can actually taste the flavor of the vegetables and herbs.

For the Slow Cooker

1. In a slow cooker, put the essential soup ingredients and steam for 8 hours on lower or 4 hours on average.

2. Over the last half-hour, place in vegetables and herbs. In the hot broth, you want to bring them a little scorching but not to mold them though you can actually taste the flavor of the vegetables and herbs.

3. Remove the chicken and cut it. Place it in the broth again.

- It's actually cheaper to purchase Thai Yellow Curry Paste than to prepare it. At your nearest Asian food store, you will find it.

- With the provided directions, prepare this in your Instant Pot or slow cooker. If required, you may use heavy whipping cream for coconut milk.

3. JALAPENO POPPER SOUP

Serving: 3

Preparation time: 25 minutes

Nutritional values: 446kcal Calories | 35g Fat | 4g Carbs | 28g Proteins

Ingredients

- 4 bacon strips

- 2 spoonful's of butter

- Medium-sized 1/2 onion, chopped

- 1/4 cup of pickled, diced jalapenos

- 2 cups broth of chicken

- 2 cups of shredded chicken, cooked

- Cream cheese 4 ounces

- Heavy cream 1/3 cup

- 1 cup of Fresh Cheddar Shredded

- 1/4 tsp. powdered garlic

- Pepper and salt, to taste

- If needed, 1/2 tsp. xanthan gum for thick soup [Optional]

Directions

1. Fry the bacon in a pan. Crumble when cooked and put aside. Place a large pot over the moderate flame while the bacon cooks. Include the onion and butter and simmer until the onion becomes porous.

2. Transfer the jalapenos and half the crumbled bacon to the pot.

3. Pour in the broth of the chicken and the shredded chicken. Take to a boil, then cook for 20 minutes, and reduce.

4. Put the cream cheese in a medium bowl and microwave for around 20 seconds; once soft until smooth, mix. Stir the cream cheese and the heavy cream into the soup. It may take a few minutes for the cream cheese to be completely integrated. Turn the heat off.

5. Include the shredded cheese, and whisk until it is completely melted. Add xanthan gum at this stage if the thick soup is preferred.

6. Serve with the leftover bacon on top.

4. PEPPERS & SAUSAGES

Serving: 6

Preparation time: 2 hrs.5 minutes

Nutritional values: 313kcal Calories | 22g Fat | 11g Carbs | 16g Proteins

Ingredients

- 1 tablespoon olive oil

- Six medium links of Pork sausage

- 3 of the large Bell peppers (cut into strips)

- 1 onion of large size (cut into half, the same size as the pepper shreds)

- Garlic 6 Cloves (minced)

- 1 tbsp. seasoning Italian

- Sea salt about 1/2 tsp.

- Black pepper 1/4 teaspoon

- 1 and a half cups of Marinara sauce

Directions

1. To activate a kitchen timer whilst you cook, toggle on the times in the directions below.

2. Heat the oil over moderate heat in a large pan. Include the sausage links until its warm. Cook on either side for around 2 minutes, only until golden brown on the outer side. (Inside, they will not be prepared.)

3. In the meantime, in a slow cooker, add the bell peppers, onions, garlic, Italian spices, salt, & pepper. Toss it to coat it. Softly spill the marinara sauce over the veggies.

4. Once the sausage links are golden brown, put them on top of the veggies in the slow cooker.

5. Cook on low flame or 2-3 hours on high flame for 4-5 hours, unless the sausages are cooked completely.

5. SHRIMPS WITH CAULIFLOWER GRITS AND ARUGULA

Serving: 4

Preparation time: 25-30 minutes

Nutritional values: 123kcal Calories | 5g Fat | 3g Carbs | 16g proteins

Ingredients

For Spicy Shrimp

- 1 pound of cleaned and roasted shrimp

- 1 tablespoon of paprika

- 2 teaspoons of powdered garlic

- 1/2 tsp. of pepper cayenne

- 1 tablespoon of olive oil extra virgin

- Salt and black pepper freshly processed

- GRITS of CAULIFLOWER

- Unsalted butter about 1 tablespoon

- Riced cauliflower about four cups

- 1cup of milk

- 1/2 cup of goat's crushed cheese

- Salt & black pepper freshly processed

For Garlic Arugula

- 1 tablespoon of olive oil extra virgin

- 3 cloves of garlic, finely minced

- 4 cups of baby arugula

- Salt & black pepper freshly processed

Directions

1. **Prepare the Spicy Shrimp:** Put the shrimp in a big plastic zip-top pack. Mix the paprika in a tiny bowl with the garlic powder as well as the cayenne to blend. Place the mixture with the shrimp into the packet and shake well before the spices have covered them. Refrigerate the grits while preparing them.

2. **Prepare the Cauliflower "Grits":** Melt the butter over a moderate flame in a wide bowl. Integrate the cauliflower rice and simmer for 2 to 3 minutes once it sheds some of its steam.

3. Whisk in half the milk and raise it to a boil. Continue to boil, stirring regularly, for 6 to 8 minutes, before some milk is consumed by the cauliflower.

4. Add the leftover milk and boil for another 10 minutes before the mixture is smooth and fluffy. Mix in the cheese from the goat and add salt and pepper. Just hold warm.

5. **Prepare Garlic Arugula:** Warm olive oil over moderate heat in a large pan. Add the garlic and simmer for 1 minute unless tangy. Include the arugula and simmer for 3 to 4 minutes, unless softened. Use salt and pepper to season, take from the pan, and put aside.

6. Heat the olive oil over low heat in the same pan. Include shrimp and simmer for 4 to 5 minutes until completely cooked. Use salt and pepper to season.

7. Divide the grits into four dishes to serve, then top each one with a fourth of the arugula & a quarter of the shrimp. Immediately serve.

6. CHICKEN CHILI WHITE

Serving: 4

Preparation time: 35-45 minutes

Nutritional values: 481kcal Calories | 30g Fat | 5g Carbs | 39g Proteins

Ingredients

- 1 lb. breast of chicken

- Chicken broth about 1.5 cups

- 2 cloves of garlic, thinly chopped

- 1 can of sliced green chills

- 1 jalapeno sliced

- 1 green pepper chopped

- 1/4 cup onion finely chopped

- Four tablespoons of butter

- 1/4 cup of heavy whipped cream

- Four-ounce cream cheese

- 2 teaspoons of cumin

- 1 teaspoon of oregano

- Cayenne 1/4 teaspoon (additional)

- To taste: salt & black pepper

Directions

1. Season the chicken with cumin, cayenne, oregano, salt, and black pepper in a wide pan.

2. Braise both sides unless golden, under medium-high heat,

3. Transfer the broth to the pan, cover, and cook for 15-20 minutes or until the chicken is completely cooked.

4. Melt the butter in a moderate pan while the chicken is frying.

5. In the pan, incorporate the chills, chopped jalapeno, green pepper, and onion, and simmer until the vegetables soften.

6. Add the chopped garlic and simmer for an extra 30 seconds, switching off the heat and put aside.

7. When the chicken is fully done, slice it with a fork and transfer it to the broth.

8. In a chicken & broth pan, incorporate the sautéed veggies and cook for 10 minutes.

9. Soften the cream cheese in the microwave in a mixing bowl so you can blend it (~20 sec)

10. Mix the cream cheese and heavy whipped cream

11. Add the mixture of chicken and vegetables into the pot and whisk rapidly.

12. Simmer for an extra 15 minutes.

13. Serve with preferred toppings such as cheese from the pepper jack, slices of avocado, coriander, sour cream.

7. BOWL OF CHICKEN ENCHILADA

Serving: 4

Preparation time: 40-50 minutes

Nutritional values: 570kcal Calories | 40g Fat | 6g Carbs | 38g Proteins

Ingredients

- 2 spoonful's of coconut oil (for searing chicken)

- 1 pound of chicken thighs that are boneless, skinless

- 3/4 cup sauce of red enchilada

- 1/4 of a cup of water

- 1/4 cup onion, minced

- 1-4 oz. green chills Can - sliced

Toppings

- 1 Avocado, sliced

- 1 cup of cheese, crushed

- 1/4 cup of pickled jalapenos, diced

- 1/2 of a cup of sour cream

- 1 tomato Roma, diced

Directions

1. Heat up the coconut oil on a moderate flame in a pan or a Dutch oven. Braise the chicken thighs unless finely brown when hot.

2. Place in the enchilada sauce as well as the water. After this, add the onion and also the green chilies. Lower the heat to a boil and cover it. Cook the chicken for 17-25 minutes or until the chicken is juicy and heated to an inner temperature of approximately 165 degrees.

3. Remove the chicken cautiously and put it on a chopping board. Then put it back into the pot. Cut or shred chicken (your preference). To retain flavor, let the chicken boil uncovered for an extra 10 minutes and enable the sauce to minimize some more.

4. For serving, cover with avocado, cheese, jalapeno, tomato, sour cream, or any other toppings you want. Feel free to adjust them to your taste. If preferred, serve individually or over cauliflower rice; just refresh your personal nutrition details as required.

8. CHIPOTLE HEALTHY KETO PULLED PORK

Serving: 10

Preparation time: 8 hrs.15 minutes

Nutritional values: 430kcal Calories | 34g Fat | 3g Carbs | 27g Proteins

Ingredients

- 1 Mid-yellow onion chopped

- 1 cup of water

- 2 tablespoons of fresh garlic diced

- 1 tablespoon of Coconut Sugar

- 1 tablespoon of salt

- 1 teaspoon of chili powder

- 1/2 teaspoon of cumin powder

- 1/2 Tablespoon Adobo sauce

- Smoked paprika 1/4 teaspoons

- 3 1/2-4 lbs. pork shoulder, Extra fat should be removed

- Whole wheat or hamburger buns without gluten OR salad wraps for serving

- Paleo ranch, to be garnished

- Coleslaw blend for optional garnish

- Lime Juice, to be garnished

- Green Tabasco for garnishing

Directions

1. Cut the onion and chop the garlic, and put it in the base of the slow cooker—a spill in a cup of water.

2. In a small bowl, mix all the ingredients for the seasoning and set it aside.

3. Slice off the pork shoulder some large, noticeable parts of fat and spread it all over with the seasoning until it is uniformly covered.

4. Over the top of the garlic, onions & water, add the pork and simmer until soft and juicy, 6-8 hours on maximum or 8-10 hours on reduced.

5. If the pork is cooked, extract much of the liquid from the crockpot and put the solids directly into the crockpot (which comprises the garlic and onions).

6. On a chopping board, move the pork and slice it with two forks.

7. In the slow cooker, shift the sliced pork back and combine with the onions and garlic. Cover unless ready to be served, and keep it warm.

8. On a bun or lettuce, place the pulled pork, served with a ranch coleslaw blend and a pinch of lime juice as well as green tabasco.

9. Enjoy.

9. STIR FRY ZOODLE

Serving: 4

Preparation time: 15-22 minutes

Nutritional values: 113kcal Calories | 3g Fat | 20g Carbs | 6g Proteins

Ingredients

- Sesame oil 11/2 tsp. (or 1 tbsp. of olive oil)

- 1 bunch of thinly chopped scallions

- 2 cloves of garlic, chopped

- 1 tablespoon of fresh ginger, diced

- Two carrots, chopped into thin strands

- One red pepper bell, cut into small strands,

- Two cups of snap peas

- Four zucchini, sliced into noodles (using a utensil like this)

- 1/4 cup of soy sauce

- 3 tbsp. vinegar for rice

- 1/4 cup of fresh cilantro, diced

Directions

1. Add the oil in a wide sauté pan over medium heat. Integrate the scallions, garlic, and ginger and simmer for 1 to 2 minutes, unless aromatic.

2. Include the bell pepper, carrots, snap peas & zucchini noodles. Sauté for 5 to 6 minutes until the vegetables just start to become soft.

3. Integrate the soy sauce & rice vinegar and proceed to cook unless the vegetables are quite soft and juicy, frequently tossing, for another 3 to 4 minutes.

4. Seasoned with cilantro, serve hot.

10. TEX MEX CHICKEN SALAD

Serving: 4

Preparation time: 25 minutes

Nutritional values: 546kcal Calories | 41g Fat | 12g Carbs | 30g Proteins

Ingredients

- For the seasoning of the fajita:
- 2 tsp. of powdered chili
- 1 tsp. of cumin
- 1 tsp. of powdered garlic
- 1 teaspoon powdered onion
- 1 tsp. of paprika. smoked
- 1/2 tsp. of or to taste salt

For the fajitas

- Two spoonful's of olive oil

- 1/2 tsp. ground mustard OR 1 tbsp. of Dijon mustard as required

- 1 lemon juice

- 2 medium breasts of chicken hammered to even density

- 2 tablespoons divided butter

- 4 finely diced medium bell peppers into slices

- 1 medium red onion finely sliced into slices

- 2-3 leaves of buttered lettuce

- 2-3 leaves of romaine lettuce

To serve

- Slices of lime

- Avocado sliced

Directions

1. Mix all the ingredients for the condiments in a tiny compostable jar. Enclose well and squish. For bell peppers, save 1 1/2 tsp.

2. Integrate two tbsp. of olive oil, lemon juice, and 5 tsp. of fajita condiments in a wide, zip lock bag. In the bag, add the chicken and secure it. Push the marinade into the chicken and enable the vegetables to marinate while preparing them (or freeze in the fridge unless ready to use).

3. Cut the bell peppers as well as onions.

4. Heat 1 tbsp. of butter over moderate heat in a large skillet. Add the onions and cook for approximately 4-5 minutes, or until tender and succulent. Transfer the bell peppers and squirt 1 1/2 tsp. of fajita condiments with the restrained ones. Cook for almost 3-5 minutes if you like the peppers with a lovely crunch. And if you like it softer, end up leaving it on for about two to three minutes long. Set aside and move to a plate.

5. Melt 1 residual tablespoon of butter and brown the chicken in the same pan. Cook for 5-6 minutes, or until properly cooked.

6. In a wide salad bowl or tray, organize the lettuce and top it with chicken as well as bell peppers. Add your chosen sliced avocados, lime slices, and any other seasonings.

11. KETO BROCCOLI CHEDDAR SOUP

Serving: 4

Preparation time: 20 minutes

Nutritional values: 285kcal Calories | 25g Fat | 3g Carbs | 12g Proteins

Ingredients

- 2 spoonful's of butter
- 1/8 cup of onion, white
- 1/2 tsp. of finely chopped garlic
- 2 cups of broth of chicken
- Pepper and salt, to taste
- 1 cup of broccoli, cut into bite-sized pieces
- 1 spoon of cream cheese
- Heavy whipping cream 1/4 cup

- 1 cup of cheddar cheese, crushed

- Bacon 2 loaves, cooked and Imploded (Optional)

- 1/2 tsp. of gum xanthan (Optional)

Directions

1. Simmer the onion and garlic with butter in a wide pot over medium heat until the onions are seamless and textured.

2. Add broth as well as broccoli to the pot. Until soft, cook broccoli. Add the salt, pepper, and seasoning you want.

3. Put the cream cheese in a medium bowl and heat for ~30 seconds in the microwave until smooth and easy to mix.

4. Mix in the soup with heavy whipping cream and cream cheese; bring to the boil.

5. Turn off the heat and mix the cheddar cheese swiftly.

6. If required, stir in the xanthan gum. Allow for stiffening.

7. Serve hot with implodes of bacon (if desired)

12. SPICY THAI BUTTERNUT SQUASH SOUP

Serving: 4

Preparation time: 30 minutes

Nutritional values: 450kcal Calories | 35g Fat | 35g Carbs | 8g proteins

Ingredients

- 11/2 tbsp. coconut oil, refined

- 1 large onion, yellow, sliced

- 1/4 cup of a paste of red curry

- One 2-inch slice of grated or finely chopped garlic

- Four teaspoons of cloves of garlic, diced

- 4 cups vegetable stock with low sodium or water

- 1 peeled and finely diced medium butternut squash (about 41/2 cups)

- One 13.5-ounce coconut milk full-fat can

- 1/4 cup cashew butter or almond butter in natural form

- Lower tamari 1 tbsp.

- 1 tablespoon maple syrup or nectar of Agave

- Kosher salt about 1 tsp., plus more to flavor

- Three teaspoons of freshly pressed lemon juice

- 1/2 cup of fresh, chopped cilantro, plus more for garnishing
- Serve with coconut yogurt, roasted peanuts, scallions & sesame seeds

Directions

1. Choose the Instant Pot Sauté mode, then add the coconut oil after several minutes. When the oil is warm, add a bit of salt to the onion, and then cook for 6 to 7 minutes before it starts to brown. Transfer the curry paste, ginger, and garlic; simmer for about 1 minute, constantly stirring, until quite tangy.

2. Spill the stock in and use a wooden spoon on the bottom of the pot to pick off some browned pieces. Stir in butternut squash, coconut milk, tamari, salt, cashew butter, and maple syrup. To blend properly, mix.

3. Shield the cover and seal the pressure release. Choose the high-pressure setting for the soup and specify the cooking time to 12 minutes.

4. Enable an organic pressure release for 5 minutes when the timer goes off, and then undergo a speedy pressure release.

5. Open the pot, add the lime juice and mix. Mix, so you have a nice and creamy broth using an electric mixer. Conversely, using a dish towel to shield the mixer cap to keep steam from spreading, you should pass the broth in batches to a mixer.

6. Stir in the minced cilantro until the broth is pureed—seasoning with coconut yogurt, peanuts, sesame seeds, and scallions as needed.

13. KETO PHO RECIPE

Serving: 4

Preparation time: 35 minutes

Nutritional values: 220kcal Calories | 5g Fat | 8g Carbs | 33g Proteins

Ingredients

- 4 Entire Star Anise

- 2 entire pods of Cardamom

- 2 entire sticks of Cinnamon

- 2 Whole Cloves

- 1 tbsp. seeds of Coriander

- 1 tsp. of ginger

- 8 cups of bone broth of beef

- 1 tablespoon of Fish sauce

- 1 tbsp. Allulose Mix of Besti Monk Fruit (optional, to taste)

- Salt (optional, to taste)

Soup Pho:

- Flank steak 12 oz. (trimmed, or sirloin)

- 2 large Zucchinis (spiraled into zoodles)

Pho toppings optional:

- Thai basil

- Cilantro

- Wedges of lime

- Slices of red chili pepper (or jalapeno peppers)

- Scallions

- Sriracha

Directions

1. For 30 minutes, put the steak in the refrigerator to make it easy to slice finely.

2. In the meantime, over moderate heat, warm a Dutch oven, minus oil. Bring the star anise, pods of cardamom, sticks of cinnamon, garlic, seeds of coriander, and fresh ginger. Toast, until aromatic, for 2-3 minutes.

3. Combine the fish sauce as well as bone broth. Mix together—Cook the pho broth and stew for 30 minutes.

4. In the meantime, to make zoodles out from the zucchini, use a spiralizer. Split the noodles from the zucchini into 4 bowls.

5. Pull it out and slice rather thinly against the grain until the steak in the refrigerator is stable. Put the steak inside each bowl on top of the zoodles.

6. Mix in the sweetener to disintegrate (if used) and modify the salt to taste whenever the broth is finished simmering. In a different pot or bowl, extract the soup. Discard all the spices that are trapped in the strainer.

7. Although the broth is already simmering, spill it over the preparing bowls instantly, making sure that the steak is immersed, so it cooks completely. (Conversely, the steak should first be stirred into the boiling broth.)

8. Thai basil, coriander, lemon slices, jalapeno or chili pepper strips, scallions, and Sriracha, and garnish with condiments of you're choosing.

14. PORK CARNITAS

Serving: 8

Preparation time: 7 hrs.15 min

Nutritional values: 442kcal Calories | 31g Fat | 9g Carbs30g Proteins

Ingredients

- 1 white, halved, and finely chopped onion
- Five cloves of garlic, chopped
- 1 jalapeño, chopped,
- 3 lbs. of cubed shoulder pork
- Salt and black pepper finely ground
- 1 tablespoon of cumin
- 2 tbsp. of fresh oregano minced
- Two Oranges
- 1 lemon
- 1/3 cup of broth of chicken

Directions

1. At the base of a slow cooker, put the onion, jalapeño garlic, pork together. Add the salt, pepper, oregano & cumin.

2. The oranges and lime are zested over the pork, then halved, and the juice is squeezed over the pork. Also, spill the broth over the pork.

3. Put the cover on and adjust the heat to medium on the slow cooker. Process for 7 hours or unless the meat is soft and quick to squash with a fork.

4. Shred the pork with two forks. The pork may be eaten instantly or frozen in an airtight jar for up to 5 days in the fridge or for up to one month in the freezer.

15. CHICKEN MEATBALLS AND CAULIFLOWER RICE WITH COCONUT HERB SAUCE

Serving: 4

Preparation time: 45 minutes

Nutritional values: 205kcal calories | 13g Fat | 3g Carbs | 20g Proteins

Ingredients

For meatballs

- Non-stick spray

- 1 tablespoon of extra virgin olive oil

- 1/2 of the red onion

- 2 cloves of garlic, chopped

- 1 lb. of ground chicken

- 1/4 cup of finely minced parsley

- 1 tablespoon of Dijon mustard

- 3/4 tsp. of kosher salt

- 1/2 tsp. of freshly ground black pepper

For sauce

- One 14-ounce of coconut milk can

- 1¼ cups of fresh, chopped parsley, distributed

- Four scallions, minced roughly

- 1 clove of garlic, peeled and crushed

- Juice and zest of one lime

- Kosher salt and black pepper, recently ground

- Red pepper flakes to serve.

- 1 Cauliflower Rice recipe

Directions

1. **Prepare the meatballs:** Set the oven to 375°F. Cover a baking sheet with aluminum foil and coat it with a non-stick spray.

2. Heat the oil in a wide skillet over medium heat. Integrate the onion and simmer until soft, about five minutes. Integrate the garlic and simmer until tangy for around 1 minute.

3. Shift the onion and garlic to a mixing saucepan and let it cool completely. Mix in chicken, parsley, and mustard, sprinkle with salt. Turn the paste into 2 tablespoon balls and shift to the parchment paper.

4. Cook the meatballs for 17 to 20 minutes until firm and fully cooked.

5. **Prepare the sauce:** In a food processor pan, blend coconut milk, scallions, parsley, garlic, lime juice & lemon zest and stir unless buttery; season with salt and pepper.

6. Cover with the red pepper flakes as well as the leftover parsley. With the sauce, end up serving over the cauliflower rice.

16. KETO RAINBOW VEGGIES AND SHEET PAN CHICKEN

Serving: 4

Preparation time: 40 minutes

Nutritional values: 380kcal Calories | 14g Fat | 35g Carbs | 31g Proteins

Ingredients

- Spray for Nonstick

- 1 lb. of boneless chicken breasts without skin

- Sesame Oil 1 tbsp.

- 2 spoonful's of soy sauce

- Honey about 2 tablespoons

- 2 bell peppers, red, chopped

- 2 bell peppers yellow, chopped

- Three carrots, diced

- 1/2 broccoli head, sliced into cloves

- 2 red, chopped onions

- Extra virgin olive oil about 2 tablespoons

- Kosher salt and black pepper, recently ground

- 1/4 cup of fresh parsley, minced, for serving

Directions

1. Heat up the oven to 400 degrees F. Slather a baking sheet lightly with non - stick spray.

2. Put the chicken on the baking tray. Stir the sesame oil and soy sauce together in a medium bowl. Dust the blend over the chicken equally.

3. On the baking dish, place the red and yellow bell peppers, broccoli, carrot & red onion. Sprinkle over the vegetables with olive oil and softly toss to coat; season with salt and pepper.

4. Roast it for 23 to 25 minutes until the veggies are soft and the chicken is thoroughly cooked. Take it out of the oven and seasoned it with parsley.

17. CAULIFLOWER POTATO SALAD

Serving: 6

Preparation time: 30-40 minutes

Nutritional values: 90kcal Calories | 4g Fat | 9g Carbs | 5g Proteins

Ingredients

- 1 head cauliflower, sliced into chunks that are bite-sized

- 3⁄4 cup of Greek yogurt

- 1⁄4 cup of sour cream

- 1 tbsp. Mustard from Dijon

- 2 tbsp. apple cider vinegar

- 1 tablespoon of fresh parsley minced

- 1 tbsp. fresh dill minced

- Celery 4 stalks, finely chopped

- 1 bunch of green, finely chopped onions

- 1/3 cup of cornichons diced

- Kosher salt and black pepper, freshly processed

Directions

1. Put the cauliflower, then coat it with water in a large container. Take the cauliflower to a simmer over moderate flame and boil until it is just fork soft, 8 to 10 minutes (do not overcook it, because, in the salad, it may not keep up).

2. Gently soak and cool the cauliflower to normal temperature. Meanwhile, mix the Greek yogurt, sour cream, mustard, vinegar, parsley, and dill together in a wide cup.

3. To incorporate, add the cauliflower, celery, green onions, and cornichons to the bowl and mix well. Sprinkle with salt & pepper.

4. When eating, chill the salad for a minimum of 1 hour. It is possible to prepare the salad 1 day in advance and keep it in the fridge until ready to eat.

18. PROSCIUTTO WRAPPED CAULIFLOWER BITES

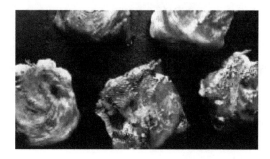

Serving: 8-10

Preparation time: 15 minutes

Nutritional values: 215kcal Calories | 15g Fat | 5g Carbs | 15g Proteins

Ingredients

- 1 tiny cauliflower

- 1⁄2 cup of paste of tomatoes

- 2 spoonful's of white wine

- 1⁄2 tsp. of black pepper

- 1⁄2 cup of Parmesan cheese grated

- 20 Prosciutto slices

- 6 tbsp. of extra-virgin olive oil

Directions

1. Start preparing the cauliflower: Cut the base, and any green leaves, away from the cauliflower. Halve the cauliflower, and slice the halves into 1-inch-thick pieces. Based on the size of the slice, divide the slices into 2 or 3 bite-size bits.

2. Bring a big saucepan of salted water to a boil. In the water, parboil the cauliflower until almost soft, for 3 to 5 minutes. With paper towels, rinse the cauliflower well enough and pat off.

3. Add the tomato paste with the white wine & black pepper in a small dish to blend. On the edges of each slice of cauliflower, distribute 1 tsp., then dust with 1 tsp. of Parmesan. A prosciutto slice is carefully wrapped over each piece of cauliflower, pushing softly at the edge to seal it (it should twig well to the tomato-paste blend).

4. Continuing to work in chunks, heat two tablespoons of olive oil over moderate heat in a large pan. Add the cauliflower while the oil is hot and simmer unless the prosciutto is crispy and golden, 3 to 4 minutes on either side. Repeat till all the pieces are ready, with extra oil and cauliflower. Let it cool slowly, then serve right away.

19. CAULIFLOWER TORTILLAS

Serving: 6

Preparation time: 45 minutes

Nutritional values: 45kcal Calories | 2g Fat | 5g Carbs | 4g Proteins

Ingredients

- 1 head cauliflower

- 2 eggs, pounded lightly

- 1⁄2 tsp. cumin

- 1⁄4 tsp. of cayenne pepper

- Salt and black pepper, freshly processed, to taste

Directions

1. Heat up the oven to 375°F. Use parchment paper to cover a baking sheet.

2. Split the cauliflower into thin strips. Cut the delicate portion of the stems roughly (discard the tough and leafy parts).

3. Move the cauliflower to the mixing bowl, filling it just halfway, working in bundles. Compress the cauliflower until it looks like rice, around 45 seconds to 1 minute. Repeat for the cauliflower that remains.

4. Move the cauliflower to a dish that is microwave-safe. Microwave around 1 minute, mix well, and microwave for an extra 1 minute.

5. Move the cauliflower to a tidy kitchen towel in the center. In a twist, cover the cauliflower up. Keep the towel over the basin and curl the ends to suck the humidity out of the cauliflower.

6. Take the cauliflower back to the bowl. Add the eggs, cumin, cayenne, salt, and black pepper, and mix well.

7. Ridge the lined baking sheet with 1/4 cup of cauliflower scoops. Distribute the cauliflower into 1/8-inch-thick circles using a tiny spoon.

8. For around 8 to 9 minutes, cook the tortillas until the bottoms are crispy. Then use a spatula to turn the tortillas over cautiously and cook for another 8 to 9 minutes unless crispy on the other side.

9. The tortillas can be eaten hot, instantly, or frozen for up to five days in an airtight jar in the fridge (with parchment pieces among them).

20. KETO SALMON SUSHI BOWL

Serving: 3-4

Preparation time: 15 minutes

Nutritional values: 45kcal Calories | 6g Fat | 8g Carbs | 9g Proteins

Ingredients

- Cauliflower Rice 3/4 Cup

- Smoked salmon about 1/2 packet

- 1/2 cup of cucumber spiraled

- Avocado 1/2

- 2 sheets of seaweed-dried

- 1 teaspoon of low sodium soy sauce

- Pepper & salt, to taste

- Wasabi 1/2 teaspoon, optional

Sauce

- 3 tbsp. mayonnaise

- Sriracha 1-2 teaspoon (adjust to preference)

Direction

1. Steam the cauliflower rice and incorporate salt and black pepper (I used premade bag)

2. Put the rice layer with soy sauce as well as seasoning in the bottom of the small dish.

3. Fill the bowl with salmon, cucumber, seaweed, and avocado

4. Integrate mayo and Sriracha for sauce, adapting to the preferred heat.

5. Spread the sauce over a dish.

6. If desired, add sesame seeds as well as pepper for garnishing.

2.3 Keto Snacks

1. BAKED GARLIC PARMESAN ZUCCHINI CHIPS

Serving: 6

Preparation time: 20-30 minutes

Nutritional values: 155kcal Calories | 10g Fat | 10g Carbs | 5g Proteins

Ingredients

- Chopped 3 to 4 zucchini into pieces of 1/4-inch and 1/2-inch

- 3 tbsp. of Omega-3 DHA Extra Virgin Olive Oil STAR

- Salt to taste and freshly ground pepper

- 1 cup bread crumbs of panko

- 1/2- cup of Parmesan grated cheese

- 1 tsp. of oregano that is dried

- 1 tsp. of powdered garlic

- Cooking spray

- Non-Fat simple yogurt, for serving,

Directions

1. Preheat the cooking oven to 450.

2. Line 3 foil-based baking sheets; brush lightly with cooking spray, then set it aside.

3. Incorporate the zucchini pieces, olive oil, salt, and pepper in a wide mixing bowl; whisk until well mixed.

4. Incorporate the crumbs, cheese, oregano, plus garlic powder in a different dish.

5. Dip the zucchini pieces in the cheese mixture and cover on both ends, press to remain with the coating.

6. On the prepared baking sheets, put the slices of zucchini in a thin layer.

7. Spray every slice lightly with cooking spray. This would help to achieve a texture that is crispier.

8. Flip the pan and finish frying for 8 - 10 mints, or until the chips are nicely browned—bake for ten min.

9. Remove it from the oven.

10. With Non-Fat Simple Yogurt, serve it.

2. KETO PIZZA ROLL-UPS

Serving: 8-10

Preparation time: 15 minutes

Nutritional values: 138kcal Calories | 12g Fat | 8g Carbs | 6g Proteins

Ingredients

- 12 mozzarella cheese slices

- Chunks of pepperoni, or you may use small pepperoni as well.

- Seasoning - Italian

- Marina Sauce - Keto

Directions

1. Heat the oven to 400°F.

2. Using a baking mat and parchment paper, cover a cookie sheet.

3. Position the slices of cheese on the baking mat, then place them in the oven for 6 mints, or unless the slices of cheese tend to brown across the corners.

4. Take it out from the oven and leave to cool the cheese moderately. If you like, make the slices to chill and scatter with Italian seasoning, as well as include pepperoni.

5. With your chosen dipping sauce, wrap & serve! Enjoy

3. STUFFED MUSHROOMS WITH SAUSAGE

Serving: 8

Preparation time: 30-40 minutes

Nutritional values: 280kcal Calories | 20g Fat | 6g Carbs | 15g Proteins

Ingredients

- 1 pound of mild Italian sausage

- Cremini mushrooms about 1 pound

- 4 ounces of cream cheese

- 1/3 cup mozzarella - shredded

- Salt, as necessary

- ½ Teaspoon flakes of red pepper

- 1/4 cup of Parmesan grated cheese

Directions

1. To 350F, set the oven. Wash and cut the stems from the mushrooms.

2. Cook the sausage in a wide skillet over moderate heat. Transfer it to a wide mixing bowl until it has been cooked.

3. Add the mozzarella cheese, cream cheese, and mix to combine. Season to taste, then add salt & red pepper if required.

4. Spoon onto the mushroom caps with the sausage combination. Use Parmesan cheese for scattering. Put in a pan or casserole platter that is oven-safe.

5. Bake for 25 mints, unless the cheese is golden brown and the mushrooms are tender.

4. EASY KETO PIZZA BITES

Serving: 30

Preparation time: 30-35 minutes

Nutritional values: 82kcal Calories | 7g Fat | 1g Carbs | 4g Proteins

Ingredients

- 1 lb., cooked as well as drained Italian sausage

- Cream cheese, 4 ounces, softened.

- 1/3 of a cup of cocoa flour

- 1/2 tsp. powder for baking

- 1 tsp. of garlic diced

- 1 tsp. of seasoning - Italian

- 3 large, beaten eggs

- 1 1/4 cup mozzarella crushed

Directions

1. Preheat the oven to 350°F.

2. Mix the prepared sausage & cream cheese unless fully fused together.

3. To give the flour time to ponder the moisture, rest of the ingredients until well mixed and cool for 10 minutes.

4. If you forget to chill the dough, they will deflate while they cook and will not be pleasant round balls.

5. Use a tiny cookie scoop to transfer onto a greased baking sheet (I prefer using the silicone baking mats).

6. Bake until lightly browned for 18-20 minutes.

7. This made 30, so it depends on the scale of the scoop you're using and how closely you're packing it.

5. CUCUMBER SLICES WITH HERB AND GARLIC CHEESE

Serving: 16

Preparation time: 5 minutes

Nutritional values: 42kcal Calories | 3g Fat | 1g Carbs | 1g Proteins

Ingredients

- 1 Diced English cucumber into 16 slices

- The Chives

- 6.5 ounces of Boursin or Alouette Herb & Garlic Cheese

Directions

1. To include some novelty, cut short slices of the cucumber skin with the help of a vegetable peeler.

2. Cut the cucumber to a thickness of around 1 mm.

3. Put the cheese in a pastry bag equipped with the edge of a large star.

4. The cucumber tips could clear every moister with a paper towel pat.

5. Puff each cucumber with the cheese and cover with a piece of chives.

6. KETO POPCORN - PUFFED CHEESE

Serving: 5

Preparation: 10 minutes

Nutritional values: 80kcal Calories | 7g Fat | 0.3g Carbs | 5g Proteins

Ingredients

- cheddar 100g/3.5 ounces

Directions

1. Slice the cheese into 0.5 inches / 1 cm pieces if you use diced cheddar. If you are using a block of cheddar, crush it to the same size using your fingertips.

2. Use a cloth/kitchen towel to wrap the cheese to keep it from being gritty and let it stay for up to 3 days in a hot, dry spot. You would like the cheese to be solid and dried absolutely.

3. Preheat oven to 390 Fahrenheit / 200 Celsius. On a baking tray covered with parchment paper, spread the cheese and bake for 4-five minutes before the cheese bursts. Put a new baking tray securely over the tray to keep it from popping out over the oven.

7. BACON WRAPPED BRUSSELS SPROUTS

Serving: 4

Preparation time: 40 minutes

Nutritional values: 170kcal Calories | 15g Fat | 3g Carbs | 2g Proteins

Ingredients

12 bacon slices

12 Brussels sprouts, cut stems

Balsamic Dip:

Mayonnaise 5 tbsp.

Balsamic vinegar about 1 tbsp.

Directions

1. Preparation: Set aside baking sheets and 12 toothpicks, covered with parchment paper or a baking mat that would be non-stick—preheat the baking oven to 400 F.

2. Wrap Sprouts: Put 1 slice of bacon on each sprout of Brussels, seal it with a toothpick, and put on the baking sheet in a thin layer.

3. Bake: Bake discovered at 400 F until the bacon is translucent and the Brussels are quite juicy around 40 minutes.

4. Serve: In a medium bowl, blend the mayonnaise & balsamic vinegar altogether unless creamy. Serve Brussels sprouts covered with bacon on a plate, along with the dip.

8. KETO ASPARAGUS FRIES

Serving: 6

Preparation time: 1hour

Nutritional values: 202kcal Calories | 14g Fat | 7g Carbs | 14g Proteins

Ingredients

- 1 pound of asparagus chopped (thick if possible)

- Salt and pepper to taste

- 1 cup of Parmesan cheese

- 3/4 cup of almond flour

- 1/4 tsp. of cayenne pepper

- 1/4 tsp. of baking powder

- 4 pounded eggs

- avocado oil spray

Directions

1. Use a fork to cut the asparagus spikes with gaps — season well with a minimum of 1/2 teaspoon of salt. Put on paper towels and let it rest for 30 minutes.

2. In the meantime, mix 1 cup of Parmesan, cayenne pepper, almond flour & baking powder in a dish. Sprinkle with salt to taste.

3. Pound the egg in a different dish.

4. Soak the asparagus segments in the eggs, then cover with the blend of the cheese.

5. Your air fryer should be preheated to 400 degrees.

6. Organize the asparagus in one layer and, if required, cook in chunks. Spray the oil well—Cook for five minutes. Turn, and then respray.

7. Fry unless the asparagus is soft for the next 4 or 5 minutes.

9. EGG, BACON, AND CHEESE SLIDERS

Serving: 6

Preparation time: 10 minutes

Nutritional values: 237kcal Calories | 18g Fat | 3g Carbs | 15g Proteins

Ingredients

- 6 peeled, boiled eggs

- 6 Thin cheddar cheese strips

- 3 Slices of bacon that has been cooked

- 1/2 of Avocado

- 1/2 teaspoon Juice of a lime

- 1/2 Teaspoon cumin

Directions

1. In a mixing bowl, place 1/2 of an avocado.

2. Stir in the cumin as well as lime juice. Mix until completely smooth. To taste, incorporate the salt.

3. Cut each hardboiled egg lengthwise in half.

4. Put on the lower half of the egg one piece of thinly cut cheddar cheese.

5. Place 1/2 a slice of cooked bacon on edge.

6. On the edge of the bacon, put a spoonful of the avocado mixture on top.

7. To make a little sandwich, place the remaining half of the egg face right over the top. Protect the bite of the egg with a toothpick placed down the center.

8. For your remaining eggs, replicate steps 4-7.

9. Add salt and pepper to each bite of the egg to taste & serve.

10. TURKEY BACON WRAP RANCH PINWHEELS

Serving: 6

Preparation time: 15 minutes

Nutritional values: 133kcal Calories | 12g Fat | 2g Carbs | 5g proteins

Ingredients

- 6 ounces of cheese cream

- 12 strips of smoked turkey deli (about 3 oz.)

- 1/4 teaspoon powdered garlic

- 1/4 teaspoon of chopped dried onion

- Dried dill weed 1/4 teaspoon

- 1 tablespoon of crumbling bacon

- 2 tablespoons cheddar shredded cheese

Directions

1. Among 2 pieces of plastic wrap, place the cream cheese. Stretch it out until it's approximately 1/4 inch thick. Scrape the plastic wrap off the top piece. On top of the cream cheese, place the slices of turkey on the edge.

2. Cover and switch the whole item over with a fresh layer of plastic wrap. Chop off the plastic bit that is on the upper right now. Slather it on top of the cream cheese with the seasoning. Spray it with cheese and bacon.

3. Roll the pinwheels up such that the exterior is the turkey. Refrigerate for 2 minimum hours. On the edge of low-carb crackers or diced cucumber, cut into 12 bits and serve.

2.4 Keto Desserts

1. KETO BROWN BUTTER PRALINES

Serving: 10

Preparation time: 16 minutes

Nutritional values: 338kcal Calories | 36g Fat | 3g Carbs | 2g Proteins

Ingredients

- 2 Salted butter sticks

- Heavy cream 2/3 cup

- 2/3 Cup of Sweetener Granular 1/2 tsp. of xanthan gum

- 2 Cups Pecans diced
- Maldon Sea salt

Directions

1. Use parchment paper or a silicone baking mat to make a cookie sheet.

2. Cook the butter in a skillet over medium flame, stirring regularly. It's going to take less than five min. Whisk in the heavy cream, sweetener, and xanthan gum. Extract it from the heat.

3. Mix in the nuts and put in the fridge, stirring regularly, for 1 hour to tighten up. The mixture's going to get really dense. Scrape onto the prepared baking sheet into 10 cookie styles and spray, if necessary, with the Maldon salt. Let the baking sheet freeze until frozen.

4. Store and keep stored in the fridge until served in an airtight dish.

2. KETO CHOCOLATE MOUSSE

Serving: 4

Preparation time: 10 minutes

Nutritional values: 220kcal Calories | 25g Fat | 5g Carbs | 2g Proteins

Ingredients

- 1 Cup of Whipped Heavy Cream

- 1/4 cup Cocoa powder unsweetened, sifted

- 1/4 Cup Sweetener Powdered

- 1 tsp. extract of vanilla

- Kosher salt about 1/4 teaspoon

Directions

1. Use the cream to whip into stiff peaks. Include the cocoa powder, vanilla, sweetener, and salt, then mix until all the products are mixed.

3. KETO CHEESECAKE FLUFF

Serving: 6

Preparation time: 10 minutes

Nutritional values: 260kcal Calories | 27g Fat | 4g Carbs | 4g Proteins

Ingredients

- 1 Cup of Whipping Heavy Cream
- 1 Eight oz. Cream Cheese Brick, Softened
- 1 Lemon Zest
- 1/2 Cup of Sweetener Granular

Directions

1. In a stand mixer, combine the heavy cream as well as stir until stiff peaks are made. A hand blender or a whisk can also be used by hand using a whisk.

2. In a different bowl, scrape the whipped cream and put it aside.

3. In the stand blender bowl, add the textured cream cheese, zest, and sweetener, then beat until sturdy.

4. With the cream cheese, add the whipped cream into the stand blender dish. Mix carefully until it is halfway mixed with a spatula. To finish whipping until sturdy, use the stand mixer.

5. Serve with a favorite topping of you.

4. LOW CARB BLUEBERRY CRISP

Serving: 2

Preparation time: 20-25 minutes

Nutritional values: 390kcal Calories | 35g Fat | 17g Carbs | 6g Proteins

Ingredients

- 1 Cup of Fresh or Frozen Blueberries

- 1/4 Cup Halves of Pecan

- Almond Meal/Flour 1/8 cup

- Butter around 2 tbsp.

- Granular Sweetener 2 tablespoons - distributed

- 1 tablespoon of flax

- Cinnamon 1/2 Teaspoon

- ½ teaspoon Extract from vanilla

- Kosher salt about 1/4 teaspoon

- Heavy cream 2 tablespoons

Directions

1. Heat the oven to 400F.

2. Put 1/2 cup of blueberries and 1/2 tablespoons of swerve sweetener in 2, 1 cup ramekins. Blend and combine.

3. Incorporate the pecans, almond flour, butter, 1 tbsp. sweetener, cinnamon, ground flax, vanilla, and kosher salt into the food processor. Pulse while you mix the ingredients.

4. Place on top of the blueberries with the blend. Put the ramekins on a baking sheet and cook for 15-20 minutes in the middle of the oven or until the topping turn's toasty brown. Serve with 1 tablespoon of heavy cream slathered on top of each one.

5. 1 MINT LOW CARB BROWNIE

Serving: 1

Preparation time: 3 minutes

Nutritional values: 196kcal Calories | 17g Fat | 2g Carbs | 8g Proteins

Ingredients

- 2 tablespoons almond flour

- 1 tablespoon of preferred granulated sweetener

- 1 tablespoon powdered cocoa

- Baking Powder 1/8 teaspoon

- Almond butter 1 tablespoon. * See notes

- 3 tablespoons of milk, unsweetened almond milk,

- 1 tablespoon of chocolate chips of preference - optional

Directions

1. A tiny microwave-protected cereal bowl or ramkin is lightly greased with cooking spray and placed aside.

2. Integrate all of your dried ingredients in a medium mixing bowl and blend well.

3. Integrate the creamy almond butter and milk in a separate bowl and mix them together. Place the wet and dry ingredients together and blend properly. Roll them through if chocolate chips are used.

4. Microwave at intervals of 30 seconds until the optimal texture has been reached. Take from the microwave then, before eating, let settle for one min.

6. KETO PEANUT BUTTER BALLS

Serving: 18

Preparation time: 20 minutes

Nutritional values: 195kcal Calories | 17g Fat | 7g Carbs | 7g Proteins

Ingredients

- 1 cup of finely diced salted peanuts (not peanut flour)

- 1 cup of peanut butter

- 1 cup of sweetener powdered, like swerve

- 8-ounce chocolate chips free from sugar

Directions

1. Combine the diced peanuts, peanut butter, and the sweetener, respectively. Distribute the 18-piece crust and mold it into balls. Put them on a baking sheet covered with wax paper. Put it in the fridge until they're cold.

2. In the oven or on top of a dual boiler, heat the chocolate chips. Mix chocolate chips in the microwave, swirling every 30 seconds till they are 75percent melted. Then stir before the remainder of it melts.

3. Soak the chocolate for each peanut butter ball and put it back on the wax paper. Until the chocolate settles, put it in the fridge.

7. WHITE CHOCOLATE PEANUT BUTTER BLONDIES

Serving: 16

Preparation time: 35 minutes

Nutritional values: 105kcal Calories | 9g Fat | 2g Carbs | 3g Proteins

Ingredients

- 1/2 cup of peanut butter

- Softened butter around 4 tablespoons

- Two Eggs

- Vanilla 1 teaspoon

- 3 tbsp. fresh cocoa butter melted

- 1/4 cup of almond flour

- 1 tablespoon of coconut flour

- 1/2 cup sweetener

- 1/4 cup of fresh cocoa butter diced

Directions

1. Preheat the baking oven to 350. Use cooking spray to cover the base of a 9 into 9 baking tray.

2. Beat the first 5 ingredients with an electric mixer until creamy. Bring the flour, sweetener, and sliced cocoa butter into the mixture. Scattered in a baking dish that has been prepared. Bake until the middle no longer jostles, and the corners are golden, for 25 minutes.

3. Cool thoroughly, and then, before slicing, chill in the freezer for 2-3 hours.

8. LOW CARB BAKED APPLES

Serving: 4

Preparation time: 20 minutes

Nutritional values: 340kcal Calories | 88g Fat | 8g Carbs | 4g Proteins

Ingredients

- 2 ounces. cheese,

- 1 oz. Walnuts or Pecans

- 4 tablespoon coconut flour

- Cinnamon 1/2 tsp.

- Vanilla extract around 1/4 teaspoon

- One tart/sour apple

To serve

- 3/4 cup of heavy whipped cream

- Vanilla extract about 1/2 teaspoon

Directions

1. Heat the oven to 175°C (350°F). In a crispy dough, mix the hot butter, diced almonds, coconut flour, cinnamon & vanilla together.

2. Wash the apple, but don't eliminate the seeds or chop it. Cut both edges off and cut 4 slices through the center portion.

3. In a greased baking dish, put the slices and place dough crumbs on top. Bake fifteen minutes or more or until light brown appears on the crumbs.

4. To a moderate bowl, incorporate heavy whipping cream as well as vanilla and whisk until soft peaks appear.

5. For a minute or two, let the apples chilled and serve with a spoonful of whipped cream.

9. FROZEN YOGURT POPSICLES

Serving: 12

Preparation time: 10mins 2hours

Nutritional values: 73kcal Calories | 60g Fat | 28g Carbs | 13g Proteins

Ingredients

- 8 oz. Mango chilled, chopped

- 8 oz. Strawberries chilled

- 1 cup of Greek full-fat yogurt

- 1/2 cup of heavy whipped cream

- 1 teaspoon extract of vanilla

Directions

1. Let the strawberries and mango defrost for 10 to 15 minutes.

2. In a mixer, place all the materials and combine until creamy.

3. End up serving as fluffy ice cream instantly or pipe into Popsicle shapes and chill for at least a few hours. If you do have an ice cream machine, it can be used, of course.

10. CHOCOLATE AVOCADO TRUFFLES

Serving: 20

Preparation time: 35 minutes

Nutritional values: 65kcal Calories | 76g Fat | 19g Carbs | 5g Proteins

Ingredients

- 1 (7 ounces.) ripe, diced avocado

- Vanilla extract about 1/2 teaspoon

- 1/2 lemon, zest

- About 1 pinch of salt

- Five ounces. Dark chocolate containing cocoa solids of at least 80 percent, finely diced

- 1 spoonful of coconut oil

- 1 tbsp. cocoa powder unsweetened

Directions

1. Use an electric mixer to mix the avocado and vanilla extract. The use of ripe avocado is necessary in order for the mixture to be fully creamy.

2. Add a tablespoon of salt and mix in the lemon zest.

3. In boiling water or oven, melt the chocolate & coconut oil.

4. Incorporate the chocolate & avocado and blend properly. Let it rest for 30 minutes in the fridge or until the batter is compact but not fully solid.

5. With your fingertips, shape little truffle balls. Likewise, use two teaspoons or a tiny scoop. Morph and roll in the cocoa powder with the hands.

11. CRUNCHY KETO BERRY MOUSSE

Serving: 8

Preparation time: 10 minutes

Nutritional values: 256kcal Calories | 26g Fat | 3g Carbs | 2g Proteins

Ingredients

- Two cups of heavy whipped cream

- Three ounces. Fresh strawberries or blueberries or raspberries

- 2 oz. Pecans diced

- 1/2 of a lime, zest

- Vanilla extract around 1/4 teaspoon

Directions

1. Drop the cream into a container and whip until soft peaks appear using a hand mixer. Towards the top, add the lime zest, then vanilla.

2. Cover the whipped cream with berries & nuts and stir thoroughly.

3. Wrap with plastic and allow for 3 or even more hours for a stable mousse to settle in the fridge. While you don't like a less firm consistency, you can also experience the dessert instantly.

Conclusion

Ketogenic' is a name for a diet that is low-carb. The concept is for you to obtain more protein and fat calories and fewer carbs. You reduce much of the carbs, such as sugar, coffee, baked goods, and white bread that are easily digestible.

If you consume fewer than 50 g of carbs a day, the body can gradually run out of resources (blood sugar) that you can use instantly. Usually, this takes 3 or 4 days. Then you're going to start breaking down fat and protein for nutrition, which will help with weight loss. This is classified as ketosis.

A ketogenic diet plan intended to induce ketosis, disintegrate body fat into ketones and enable the body to perform on ketones instead of glucose to a great extent. Since samen is the ultimate aim of these diets, there are typically a lot of connections between the various forms of the ketogenic diet, especially in terms of being low in carbohydrates and high in dietary fat. A program that focuses on high-fat and low carbohydrates is the Ketogenic Diet, and it has many advantages.

It is necessary to remember that a short-term diet that emphasizes weight reduction rather than medical benefits is a ketogenic diet. To reduce weight, people use a keto diet more commonly, although it may help treat some medical problems, such as epilepsy, too. People with heart problems, some neurological disorders, and also acne can even be supported, although further research in those fields needs to be conducted.

CPSIA information can be obtained
at www.ICGtesting.com
Printed in the USA
BVHW051800050421
604209BV00009B/574